Building Strong Communities

Building Strong Communities

Guidelines on empowering the grass roots

STEVE SKINNER

BLOOMSBURY ACADEMIC
LONDON • NEW YORK • OXFORD • NEW DELHI • SYDNEY

BLOOMSBURY ACADEMIC
Bloomsbury Publishing Plc
50 Bedford Square, London, WC1B 3DP, UK
1385 Broadway, New York, NY 10018, USA
29 Earlsfort Terrace, Dublin 2, Ireland

BLOOMSBURY, BLOOMSBURY ACADEMIC and the Diana logo
are trademarks of Bloomsbury Publishing Plc

First published 2020 by RED GLOBE PRESS

Reprinted by Bloomsbury Academic

Copyright © Steve Skinner, under exclusive license to Springer Nature Limited 2020

Steve Skinner has asserted his right under the Copyright,
Designs and Patents Act, 1988, to be identified as the author of this work.

For legal purposes the Acknowledgements on p. xii-xiii constitute
an extension of this copyright page.

A catalogue record for this book is available from the British Library.

A catalog record for this book is available from the Library of Congress.

ISBN: PB: 978-1-3520-0785-5
ePDF: 978-1-3520-0786-2
ePub: 978-1-3503-1323-1

To find out more about our authors and books visit
www.bloomsbury.com and sign up for our newsletters.

For Sandra

Contents

6   A Partnership Approach   139

Chapter 6 looks at the roles public sector organisations can play to work in partnership with the community and voluntary sectors in strengthening communities. It describes the key elements of a strategic approach to strengthening communities.

This book introduces a definition of the term 'strong communities' with seven key features: *Active, Organised, Participative, Resourceful, Accepting, Connected and Fair*. The material focuses on the first three of these seven features, because the author's experience is mostly in these areas and because to address all seven features would need at least two publications. It draws on a community development approach, but places this in the current climate and the context of building stronger communities.

Preface

This book is a resource for strengthening communities. It contains guidelines, frameworks and a range of approaches to help plan and implement effective community support.

The book is written by a practitioner for other practitioners, combining both theory and practice. It draws on recent research and uses many practical examples from around the UK, as well as several from Yorkshire, where the author is based. A key focus of this book is on 'empowering the grass roots'. The term 'grass roots' is used broadly to mean the voluntary and community sectors, with an emphasis on the community sector, as explained below. Resource One at the end of the book gives definitions of key terms used.

The art of strengthening communities is explored around four themes: *Building People*, *Building Organisations*, *Building Involvement* and *Building Equality*. These themes are examined in turn in the next four chapters. Used in combination, these themes can provide a useful, comprehensive framework for understanding the practical aspects of strengthening communities.

Through discussing these themes, the book describes a wide range of approaches, methods and tools to use with communities, with references and links, wherever possible, for you to find out more. Chapter 4 introduces a new model called the Wheel of Participation, which can help community groups to make informed choices about their future direction. Chapter 5 explores the vital issues around diversity, inclusion and equal opportunities and how they affect building stronger communities. Public services and larger 'infrastructure' voluntary organisations, providing support to voluntary and community groups, also have key roles to play, as discussed in Chapter 6.

The book has been written for people based in a broad range of settings, such as members of community groups, active residents and local leaders. It will also be helpful for staff and managers based in the public sector who are running front-line services or responsible for area management. In addition, it hopefully will be valuable for community workers, consultants and campaigners, and staff in private sector organisations involved in corporate social responsibility. Trustees, volunteers and staff in voluntary organisations and elected members in district, borough, county, town and parish councils will also find the book useful.

The material will also be a resource for participants of professional training programmes and students in higher education in a range of disciplines, including social work, housing management, community health, adult education, community development, social enterprise and local government studies.

For the sake of brevity, the term 'community practitioner' is used in this book for people in all these different roles, whether paid or unpaid, full time or part time, where the person is committed to strengthening communities. Obviously, each context will have its own challenges and opportunities. Finally, it will also be useful for policy-makers in the voluntary and public sectors, and in both central and local government, to inform strategic planning for strengthening communities.

The book contains examples of practical methods, though it is mainly not intended as a training manual or a handbook. It acts as an introduction to a range of approaches, where the main aim is to build stronger communities through supporting conscious, skilful practice in and with communities, based on a clear set of values. Each chapter finishes with some questions that you might find useful to consider when working with communities.

It is appreciated that your response to this book and the issues you need to consider will vary depending on your role: whether you are an officer in a local authority, the leader of a community group, a student on a course or a voluntary sector-based project organiser. In using the material in this book with communities, please bear in mind that, as practitioners, we cannot force changes on individuals, groups and networks; the interest in development and change needs to come from communities themselves. Whatever the setting of the practitioner, the work of strengthening communities also needs to be informed by particular values. Consequently, at various points in this publication, several of the values underlying the work, and the challenges they pose, are discussed.

In using the approaches and methods described in this book, practitioners need to be aware of the challenging social climate that many areas are now experiencing, as discussed in Chapter 1. However, this book also looks ahead to the longer term, in order to make a contribution to building a fairer and more participative society.

About the Author

Steve Skinner, MA, CQSW, is an experienced community practitioner who specialises in community engagement, organisational change and leadership, working throughout the UK. He was formerly the Policy Manager for Community Development in Bradford Council and a Regional Manager for the Community Development Foundation. He now works directly with community groups, voluntary organisations, partnerships and councils, providing services in training, consultancy and evaluation, and has a track record as an author and conference speaker. Outside of his community development work, he is a singer-songwriter in a touring duo.

Author's Acknowledgements

With warm thanks for the help, ideas and information provided by many people and organisations in writing this publication:

Matt Leach, The Local Trust

Niamh Goggin, Small Change Limited

Ben Lee, The National Association for Neighbourhood Management

Dr Pawda Tjoa, New Local Government Network

Elizabeth Chamberlain, National Council for Voluntary Organisations

Jeff Scales, Locality

Paul Nagle, ShedNet

Amanda Stevens, The National Association for Voluntary and Community
Action (NAVCA)

Helen Clay and Laura Jamieson, LeftCoast

Kate Kershaw, Super Slow Way

Amjid Hussain, UnLtd

Stuart Hashagen, Susan Paxton and Fiona Garven, The Scottish
Community Development Centre

Chrissie Cahil, The Community Foundation for Northern Ireland

Dave Morgan, Third Sector Projects

Karen Davies, Purple Shoots

Noel Mathias and Josephine McLaughlin, WEvolution

Thanks for comments and contributions from:

Alison Gilchrist, Mandy Wilson, Guy Farrar, Max Farrar, Richard Norbury, Alan Anderton, Liz Richardson, Ed Carlisle, Alana Gooding, Jim Boot, Chris Church, Paul Nagle, Jim Boot, Anne Timms, Janine Ward and Brian Player.

The text on social media is based on contributions from Sandra Twitchett, Guy Farrar and Maxine Moar.

Text in Box 2.8 and on *Using Freire's approach in Lancashire*, in Chapter 2, is based on material provided by Robert Waller and Yasmeen Ali from the

University of Central Lancashire's Centre for Volunteering and Community Leadership.

Thanks for extensive comments and contributions from David Wilcox, Sandra Twitchett, Stuart Hashagen and Gabriel Chanan.

Special thanks to Alan Twelvetrees for his support, comments, contributions and guidance.

In addition to the above individuals and organisations, thanks to the following for providing examples:

CNet, Bradford

Barnsley Metropolitan Borough Council

The London Borough of Hackney

Threeways, Halifax

Space 4 Impact, South Africa

The Thornbury Centre, Bradford

Creative People and Places

The Adult Learning Project, Edinburgh

Blackburn Healthy Living

Little Hulton Big Local, Salford

1

Introduction

In the current climate, many communities across the UK are facing increased tensions and divisions. This has been caused over the last few years by a variety of factors, including insecurities around Brexit, the implementation of austerity policies, the media's focus on migrants and refugees, and a tragic series of extremist attacks (Jones et al., 2017). Although austerity is officially over as a policy and, at time of writing, the current government is announcing new spending plans, many public services are still having to manage on years of reduced resources. Associated with this, funding for the voluntary and community sectors has declined, for both front-line services and for the supporting infrastructure. Public sector grants to community groups and voluntary organisations have been widely replaced by competitive procurement, involving demanding processes for smaller charities and community groups (Select Committee on Charities, 2017).

As well as this reduction of support, and the loss of posts dedicated to community engagement, there has been greater reliance by councils on volunteering and community self-help, with the well-worn expectation in many cases that such initiatives can help to maintain service levels normally provided by the public sector (Berner and Philips, 2008). In this context of reduced support, voluntary and community organisations have had to cope with higher levels of demand. They are often taking initiatives to diversify their income sources, and, in some cases, have been forced into artificial partnerships of which they would rather not be a part. Equally, many community groups are reviewing their traditional roles, are taking on new challenges and are keen to build wider relationships.

In this changing and demanding context, social media have increasingly become available as a tool in community engagement, providing new ways for people to get involved in their areas. The pattern of actual use of such media by community groups, however, still appears to be patchy (Harris and McCabe, 2017). Legislation in different parts of the UK has provided some new mechanisms for communities to have greater participation. For instance, the Localism Act of 2011 provided a number of opportunities for communities in England to have greater influence on local issues, such as land use and the purchase of local assets, although research has questioned the impact of this (Locality, 2017). In Wales, the passing of the Well-being of Future Generations Act of 2015 required, among other things, public bodies to work better with communities. In Scotland, the introduction of the Community Empowerment Act in 2015 provided additional ways for communities to have influence on service design and delivery. The material in this book needs to be adapted to these differing contexts.

The Equality Act of 2010 made it illegal across the UK to discriminate against anyone because of one of the 'protected characteristics', which are age, disability, sex, gender reassignment, marriage and civil partnership, pregnancy and maternity, race, religion or belief, and sexual orientation. In August 2018, the Government launched a new strategy, *Civil Society Strategy: Building a Future that Works for Everyone* (HM Government, 2018), though, at time of writing, it is hard to describe any likely outcomes arising from this initiative.

So, while there are new opportunities in some cases, the changes described above which are associated with the current climate are mainly having negative impacts on communities, especially in deprived areas. Overall, many communities in Britain face grim levels of deprivation. According to recent research, 1.5 million people, including 365,000 children, were destitute in the UK at some point during 2017 (Fitzpatrick et al., 2018). In 2017, 14 million people, one-fifth of the population, lived in poverty. Four million of these were more than 50% below the poverty line (Alston, 2018). Some minorities are experiencing increased levels of discrimination and face barriers to their active involvement in community life. Consequently, strengthening communities needs to be planned, resourced and implemented with an awareness of this challenging economic and social climate.

Part One: The aim – strong communities

In building stronger communities, it is useful to have a description of what *strong communities* could look like. Strong communities could be described as having the following seven features:

> - *Active* – where people are involved in local activities, where they care about their community and are engaged in community action to improve the quality of life.

> - *Organised* – where people come together to form and sustain groups, networks and organisations that run community activities, address common needs and provide local services.

> - *Participative* – where people and groups contribute to decisions that affect their lives and have a real say about the issues that concern them.

➤ *Resourceful* – where existing skills and assets are recognised and used, where learning is valued, within a creative and enterprising environment.

➤ *Accepting* – where people are accepting of each other, with an understanding of different cultures, traditions and beliefs, and where a diversity of backgrounds is valued.

➤ *Connected* – where a sense of belonging exists; people and groups from different backgrounds have places and spaces to meet, contact and communicate with each other and, where appropriate, there is joint working between different groups.

➤ *Fair* – where people from different backgrounds and identities have a similar level of opportunities, with equal access to services and resources; where social injustice and discrimination are actively challenged.

This definition, based on seven key features, intentionally uses everyday language and attempts to address issues that are important to communities. For example, a recent study based on a sample of over 10,000 adults, identified the high level of concern for 'fairness' (Knight, 2015). Communities being *'active'*, in many cases, can mean people simply getting together for local activities, such as a social evening in the community centre or a night at the bingo. Such small-scale, self-organised activities are important in many communities, and significant for generating informal community support.

From this definition of strong communities, the work of strengthening communities will involve working with:

➤ *Individuals* – volunteers, active residents, group and network members, service users, campaigners, community representatives and local leaders, so that they are confident, well informed, skilful and effective (Chapter 2).

➤ *Local groups and organisations* – community groups, voluntary organisations, networks, clubs, online groups and community enterprises, so that they are well-organised and achieving their aims (Chapter 3). Those building stronger communities will also need to consider the pathways groups are choosing to achieve their aims. This is explored using the new Wheel of Participation (Chapter 4).

➤ *Public and private sector organisations* – such as local authorities, health service providers, police forces, housing associations and locally based companies, so that they actively support the strengthening of communities (Chapter 5).

When consulted about the term 'strong communities', some people described it as a place with access to jobs, education, recreation, care, a secure home, a decent environment and similar elements (SCDC, 2012). However, the focus of this publication is more on the nature of community life, described by the seven features as introduced above, rather than the environmental, economic or educational aspects of stronger communities. Having said that, the seven key features may be interpreted in diverse ways by different groups in the community. Such differing perspectives need to be respected and considered by practitioners in their work on strengthening communities.

Different communities will display varying levels of the seven features; whatever the starting point, an asset-based approach, as explained below, is about recognising and building on what already exists.

Box 1.1 Outcomes arising from stronger communities

Increased *resilience* can be seen as an outcome of the process of strengthening communities. The term can describe where communities are able to cope well and respond to change, hazards and negative impacts in constructive ways (Walker, 2015). Although as a term it is sometimes used interchangeably with the term 'strong communities', in this publication it is seen as an *outcome* arising from stronger communities, especially associated with them being better *connected* and more *organised*. Bear in mind, the term *resilience* used in this context is complex, in that it has a variety of meanings; for example, it has also been used in environmental initiatives to describe the relationship between healthy functioning eco-systems and social well-being (WCVA, 2017). As a term, it has also been used in the Home Office's *Stronger Britain Together* programme, initiated in 2016. This policy is part of a long-standing concern by different governments to promote greater community cohesion.

A second proposed outcome arising from stronger communities is higher levels of social capital. Social capital can be described as a situation where:

'People are connected with one another through intermediate social structures – webs of association and shared understandings of how to behave. This social fabric greatly affects with whom, and how, we interact and co-operate. It is this everyday fabric of connection and tacit co-operation that the concept of social capital is intended to capture.'

(Halpern, 2005, p. 3)

While the link between civic engagement and increased social capital has been contested (Foley and Edwards, 1999), the concept of social capital has become increasingly popular among policy-makers, including, for example, the HM Treasury. Social capital, according to one influential writer, is the bedrock of relationships and collective activity, in particular involving 'bonds and bridges' between people to provide a platform for social support (Putman, 2000). Using the proposed definition of 'strong communities', it seems likely that the features of being *active* and *connected* will contribute to building social capital, for example, where people are involved in informal activities and groups, and where trust and connections can be built. Other outcomes of strong communities are described in a policy document published recently by central government (Ministry of Housing, Communities and Local Government, 2019).

What does the term *community* mean?

Practitioners need to be aware of different interpretations of the term 'community' as it will influence their work with individuals, networks and groups. It is a complex term, with a long history of analysis (Farrar, 2002); a major piece of research in the 1950s revealed there were 94 different meanings to the term! (Hillery, 1955).

Understanding the term can be based around a number of questions, as follows:

➣ *Is it about shared characteristics?* These could be class, gender, age, or use of services or circumstances, such as being parents or being unemployed. For instance, research on traditional, white, working-class areas in Middlesborough indicated a strong sense of solidarity among residents through their position in the labour market (MacDonald et al., 2005). However, where such shared characteristics are strongly present, this can make acceptance of people with different characteristics more difficult.

➣ *Is it about a sense of belonging?* This can be through a strong attachment to place, for example, through living in a street for a long time. However, a strong sense of belonging may be rather exclusive, for example, through ownership of property or at worst, a strong sense of territoriality where local gangs perceive they 'own' their estate.

➣ *Are communities networks?* Communities can be seen as networks, involving mutual trust and shared obligations. However, it can be argued that just because a person is in a network, they are not necessarily in a community, as is the case in many online 'networks'.

'Community therefore is something that can be expressed through networks of sociability, but it is not necessarily to be identified with such networks.'

(Somerville, 2011, p. 3).

➣ *Is it an ideal?* There are also underlying beliefs and hopes people may have about the term 'community' and its symbolic mesaning. For instance, some people in the UK hark back to earlier times, believing that in the past, there was a greater sense of community. Equally the concept of community can be used to describe some future vision and inspire people to work towards an ideal state. This may happen locally, but can also occur at national levels (Anderson, 1983). It can be based on left or right political values and, for some communities, be based on religious beliefs (Farrar, 2002). The ideal of 'community' can also have its negative side, where it is used to strengthen fears and prejudice some social groups may hold against others and be used to justify these groups' exclusion (Young, 1990).

➤ *Is it a call to action?* This is where individuals feel obliged to act in certain ways (Butcher, 1993). For instance, householders may feel obliged to keep their front gardens tidy and not leave rubbish littering the pavement. Obligations can be positive or negative, where people feel they must conform in order to be accepted. Such obligations can be unspoken and informal or more formally and explicitly presented, such as where police advise house-holders on crime prevention (Somerville, 2011).

➤ *Is it about connections between people?* Being connected is different from having a sense of belonging The key issue here is that the connections are *meaningful* in some way. How people are connected with each other, so that it feels meaningful, will vary depending on their particular circumstance and setting. Connections can be weak or strong; strong connections, for example, can arise from extended family relationships or close cultural identities. Such ties can be positive or negative – negative in the sense that they can lead to domination of a person's behaviour, such as women being kept in traditional domestic roles against their preference. So, it is crucial to bear in mind that such close ties may not always be positive. *Being connected* is one of the seven key features of a strong communities; consequently, the concept of *meaningful connections,* where they are positive, is especially useful for practitioners.

'Community is about connectedness among persons, and the connectedness has to be meaningful to the persons concerned – there has to be a substantive grouping or collectivity with which those persons can be identified (by themselves or by others), with the possibility of recognition of one another as being members of it.'

(Somerville, 2011, p. 7)

Communities of place and interest

An important perspective is that the term 'communities' is more appropriate than the term 'community'; in practice, areas are often made up of a combination of different cultures, attachments and identities. Communities can be described as having at least two different aspects, *communities of place* and *communities of interest,* and these are now discussed in turn. The term *communities of place* is useful where people share a location, such as a village, street, neighbourhood, town, city or borough. In using this term to describe some types of communities, there are a number of issues to consider. Firstly, while superficially appearing straightforward, the term 'communities of place' raises the question of who defines the geographical area involved (Farrar, 2002). Is it defined by the inhabitants or by some external authority? For instance, this question was an issue in drawing boundaries for some of the New Deal for

Communities regeneration areas. In addition, different groups may have different concepts of their territory; a local street gang might have a different area they identify with compared to a large community association. For some residents, their local community might be just their street (Hay, 2008). Any one resident may have several layers of attachment to place, ranging from their street to their village, the whole town or the whole district.

While the term 'communities of place' is useful, there are many limitations associated with it. Sharing the same place to live does not necessarily mean people feel they are part of a community. Some communities of place may define themselves as being strongly associated with defined geographical features, such as a valley, while others may have loose boundaries and not actually mean much as a basis of interaction and involvement.

Communities of interest, in contrast, can be described as people who share:

> ➤ an *interest,* such as a particular sport;

> ➤ an *experience,* such as refugees;

> ➤ a *concern,* such as carers; or

> ➤ an *identity,* such as belonging to a faith or ethnic group.

Some communities of interest overlap with or can be based in a community of place, such as a Jewish community living in one specific city neighbourhood. Equally, some communities of interest are spread out across a city or region without any geographical focus. Rather than based on where people live, people's identity may be more based on their faith, their disability, their sexuality or where they came from, such as a particular island in the Caribbean (Hudson et al., 2007). The term 'communities of interest' has been a useful tool to help consider the needs of excluded and marginalised groups.

More generally, in using the term 'communities of interest', there are a number of issues to consider. Firstly, just because a person is a refugee, it does not necessarily mean they are part of a community of refugees. As explored above, being part of a community requires some other dynamics, such as a sense of meaningful connection. Secondly, how far does the term 'communities of interest' extend? The term is lacking clear definition; is a sports group, such as a golf club, a community of interest? The term has been used in work with communities to include such a broad range of interests. However, in practice, the term 'communities of interest' is generally intended to mean a social group that experiences discrimination or is marginalised in some way (Pugh, 2003). One further criticism of the focus on communities of interest is that it has diverted attention away from a focus on place, in other words, away from the lack of allocation of the state's resources to poor areas.

Despite these reservations, the concepts of communities of interest and communities of place both contribute to understanding the process of building stronger communities. Different types of communities will have differing priorities between the proposed seven key features of strong communities. Any one person could be involved in two or three different communities simultaneously, and not want to be labelled as solely 'local', 'gay' or 'disabled'. People's attachment to these different identities will often also grow and change over time.

An additional, widely used and useful term is *communities of identity*. As shown above, people who share an identity, such as a faith or ethnicity, is included as part of the description of communities of interest, though the term 'communities of identity' is also often used separately. The growing movement in the UK involving people claiming their rights based on their identity has been very important for minorities to gain confidence and recognition of the discrimination they face. Increasingly identities are being seen as multi-layered and interacting with each other – a black women's experience of discrimination may be different from that experienced by a woman with a disability. This important concept is called *intersectionality* (Shaw and Mayo, 2016). According to some writers, there was a failure by practitioners until the 1990s to recognise that people with disabilities also have identities as men and women, black or white people and other categories (Ramcharan et al., 1997).

Often a newly added element in describing communities is the term *communities online* – where people form relationships through social media networks. With this new concept of communities online, there is a valid question whether the use of social media is facilitating new relationships that are substantially different in nature from those already existing in communities of interest and communities of place or is just a new medium for essentially similar types of contact and connections. For example, an online network called Nextdoor is used by over 14,000 neighbourhoods across the country. The network helps people get in touch with other residents in their area for information on tradespeople, discussion on safety issues, planning local events and posting items for sale. Its membership is based on location, so such interaction could be viewed as communities of place using social media to communicate more effectively. However, the interactions of some groups of people, for example, those participating in video games online, presumably indicates forms of association that would not exist outside the internet. A key question is whether these function as communities, rather than interactions between people, without any meaningful connection. While there are many new opportunities, there has been a lack of research to identify what 'community engagement' actually means in the context of social media, and how it might be measured; is it reduced, in some cases, to a series of clicks on a keyboard? Despite its great potential, there has been non-use and lapsed use of social media by community groups and smaller voluntary organisa-tions (Harris and McCabe, 2017). A further question is: By getting involved in online networking, does that reduce the level of involvement of people in more direct, face-to-face forms of participation or increase it? A lack of litera-ture on this type of issue prevents any clear indication of trends (Harris and McCabe, 2017).

Some writers argue there is no agreed definition of 'community' (Farrar, 2002). For an interesting discussion on the rather complex issues associated with the terms, see Somerville (2011).

Finally, as well as communities of place and communities of interest, there is a major question as to whether wealth or class should be used as a way of describing communities, a concept discussed in earlier decades (Boudier, 1984). In modern, divided Britain, with many areas facing harsh levels of dep-rivation alongside extreme affluence for some, the concept of 'communities of income' may be useful to describe the reality of how some groups form links and relationships. This also relates to the concept of 'social capital' and how poorer communities may have reduced levels of 'bridging' relationships (Halpern, 2005; Putman, 2000). The concept of communities of interest has been a valuable tool to better understand how communities work in modern Britain. However, some writers argue that a critical understanding of class is fundamental to understanding the term 'communities' (Mae and Mayo, 2016).

Bearing these considerations in mind, the different ways of describing communities discussed in this chapter can be useful for practitioners who are working with different groups and getting people involved. In particular, building *meaningful connections* seems a useful concept to inform the work of strengthening communities and directly relates to the features of being *active* and *connected,* two of the seven key features of strong communities intro-duced earlier. The aim of this brief introduction to the meaning of community and communities has been to make practitioners more aware of some of the key debates and difficulties in using the terms.

Box 1.2 Asset-based community development

The approaches used in this book are informed partly by what is known as asset-based community development. ABCD is a way of working with communities that starts from the skills, talents and abilities of people at the grass roots, focusing on assets and strengths, rather than on needs and problems. The ABCD approach val-ues the key roles played by community groups and organisations, both informally and formally organised. One method of ABCD is called the 'community building' process (Kretzmann and McKnight, 1993). An early stage in community building involves a

▶

◄

scoping exercise to identify local assets, which, as well as individual skills and local
groups, also includes physical features of the area, such as parks, rivers, public buildings and green spaces. The community building approach also includes 'institutions',
such as schools, colleges, public services, housing associations and businesses.
The connections that exist between residents are a key focus to build on, and the
emphasis is on self-help. While having its own dilemmas, as discussed later, ABCD
is an important approach to consider in the policy and practice work of strengthening
communities.

Part Two: The process – community empowerment

Many public services, voluntary organisations and community groups are
interested in the idea of *community empowerment*. 'Community empowerment' is a widely used term, though in practice rarely defined; many practitioners feel passionately committed to empowering people but have never
really considered what it actually means! It is often used as a vague, rather
romanticised concept and is in need of clarification. It can be understood in a
number of ways, such as communities:

➤ *having influence* over local decisions

➤ *taking action* to improve the quality of their lives

➤ *being valued* for their skills, talents and abilities

➤ *feeling confident,* with high levels of self-belief

➤ *accessing resources* that improve people's quality of life

➤ *understanding* the causes of discrimination and deprivation

➤ *sharing* power, such as where community representatives join a strategic
  city-wide body

➤ *taking power,* such as where a community group takes direct action to
  overturn a local authority's planning decision.

To some extent these are overlapping concepts, though all of them are important as they might inform how practitioners work with communities. These
different ways of looking at community empowerment are now explored in
turn. The idea of empowerment as communities *having influence* on decisions
that affect their lives is a well-established view (McArdle, 1989). It relates
directly to one of the key features of strong communities given above: *'Participative – people and groups contribute to decisions that affect their lives.'* This

understanding of empowerment can be seen in government policy. For example, in 2009, the Scottish Government defined *community empowerment* as:

'A process where people work together to make change happen in their communities by having more power and influence over what matters to them.'

(The Scottish Government, 2009)

Self-help and locally based independent organising, where people *take action* themselves and do not rely on outside agencies for funding or support, has appealed to many activists as an empowering process. Here the focus is on getting on with practical actions, rather than appealing to external agencies for funding or other solutions. It can promote a 'we are all in it together' form of solidarity and be a powerful experience for participants. *Being valued* is important; appreciating people's abilities can be very supportive, especially in communities in deprived areas that have faced a stream of publicity highlighting the problems. In contrast, recognising and valuing people's existing skills and talents and the positive aspects of a neighbourhood, can be seen as an empowering approach to working with communities (Kretzmann and McKnight, 1993).

Alternatively, empowerment can be viewed partly as a psychological process of gaining personal *confidence* (Yeung, 2011). This ethos is especially linked to the women's movement of the 1970s and 1980s (Taylor, 2003), as well as assertiveness training (Back and Back, 2005).

'Empowerment is about doing things others around you do not expect you to do.'

(Community Projects Worker, Bradford)

The self-advocacy movement for people with learning difficulties has been an important opportunity for people to feel more confident and empowered (Ramcharan et al., 1997). Rather than focus on personal aspects, a different angle is empowerment as a process of *accessing resources,* a view that has been promoted by some commentators (Somerville, 2011). In order to access resources effectively it depends partly on the capacity of the community to do this; some neighbourhoods, with a low level of community organisation and leadership, have struggled to access grants, manage buildings and win campaigns.

In contrast, another key perspective is that empowerment is about *understanding* the world around us, and the underlying causes of deprivation and exclusion:

'Empowerment involves a form of critical education that encourages people to question their reality; this is the basis of collective action and is built on the principles of participatory democracy.'

(Ledwith, 2011, p. 3)

This approach draws on the work of Paulo Freire, a major thinker about radical education and the nature of empowerment (Freire, 1972); examples of using his approach are given in Chapter 2.

Finally, a major criticism of many perspectives on empowerment is that they lack an awareness of power issues. For example, a criticism of building confidence as the main emphasis in community empowerment is that it misses recognition of the role played by power in the community. Individuals might feel personally empowered, but little changes in terms of influencing the major decisions made about their community.

Box 1.3 Understanding power

Understanding the power aspect of community empowerment requires considering three key theories of power: structuralist, pluralist and transformative (Taylor, 2003).

- A *structuralist* view is where power is seen as being held by a layer of powerful organisations and individuals, who maintain their privileges as a dominant group through control of resources and policy-making. From this perspective, cultural norms and education act as ways to maintain the status quo; the elite will hang on to their power and resort to violence, if needed, to keep hold of their privileges. A structuralist position in relation to power is likely to lead to a conflict-based strategy to achieve change, an 'us and them' approach to community involvement.

- Alternatively, a *pluralist* view sees power as more spread out and de-centralised, that can be accessed and shared in a competitive manner Within the pluralist perspective, there is scope for persuasion and negotiation in order to achieve change; the 'them' of the 'us and them' are more distributed, less coordinated and less oppressive than as described in the structuralist model. How these structuralist and pluralist arrangements are maintained by elites has been examined by writers such as Gramsci and Foucault (discussed in Taylor, 2003). Both the structuralist and the pluralist perspectives are based on the assumption that power is a finite resource of limited availability – this is called the 'zero-sum' view of power (Taylor, 2003).

- In contrast, a *transformative* view sees power as more fluid in nature, where it can be built and expanded as a resource, rather than just gained or shared. Rather than power being viewed as a finite and limited resource that different groups and interests hold for themselves and compete for, a different view is that power can be generated and expanded, and is seen as open ended (Taylor, 2003). Some elected members of local authorities, for example, welcome the growth of well-organised community groups and effective community leaders, seeing these as adding to the overall level of community influence in their wards, rather than as a threat to their status and role.

▶

◀

This brief introduction to three theories of power suggests the issue is crucial for practitioners to consider as part of their work. The three themes are useful as they unearth that the different positions on power are active in communities and influence people's attitudes and behaviour.

Increased levels of empowerment will often be a journey through several of the different processes described above. Some people start by being focused on their personal needs, and then, through their experiences over time, broaden their interests onto a wider range of issues (Miller et al., 1995).

This discussion has briefly looked at different interpretations of the term 'community empowerment', and these raise a number of wider concerns:

➤ *Can empowerment as a concept be mis-used by authorities?* For instance, is the term 'community empowerment' being employed to encourage people to provide their own services, rather than receive properly funded services from public funds (Craig and Mayo, 1995)? Empowerment can be presented by local authorities as a positive policy for community involvement, such as in promoting volunteering schemes, when in practice it means asking volunteers to carry out roles formerly done by paid staff who have lost their jobs because of the austerity agenda of central government.

A more positive approach, based on five key principles, is described in a recent publication by Scotland Audit (2019)

➤ *Who is being empowered?* For example, is it already well-established groups on an estate who gain further access to funding and services? Will middle-class neighbourhoods become more empowered at the cost of other, poorer areas losing out? Do older, male members of a group benefit from a training course and still exclude women from decision-making and leadership roles? (Constantino-David, 1995).

➤ *Is personal empowerment a diversion from the real issues?* Do people feel more confident and contribute to local decisions, but still face grinding poverty? Is having a say about local services even a diversion from the real underlying issue of the overall level of available resources?

> 'We now have a larger say about how the cake is divided,
> but the cake still remains too small!'
>
> (Community activist, Bradford)

➤ *Will empowerment programmes be challenged by local leaders?* In some cases, local leaders benefit from their existing positions of influence and status and may feel threatened by initiatives that give others greater influence and impact. Some elected members in local authorities may react in this way, an issue discussed later in this chapter.

These questions touch on real issues that exist in communities. This book argues that, despite these difficulties, community empowerment needs to be part of the process of strengthening communities, as described in the next four chapters. It needs to be real – to be based in the reality of people's lives, based on the poverty and exclusion faced daily by many and the demands of challenging the status quo. In this publication, community empowerment is not seen as an end in its own right, but part of the process of building stronger communities, and needs to be informed by a set of values, as discussed in Chapter 5.

So far, we have just begun to identify some of the issues and challenges associated with the term 'community empowerment'. A final and crucial question is:

> *Can empowerment ever be given to communities?* Is it more about communities being supported to discover, release and win their own power? (Eade and Williams, 1995). This is a crucial point; that in the process of strengthening communities, practitioners cannot give anyone empowerment but can help to create opportunities and situations where communities can discover, experience and fight for their own empowerment.

'By its very nature empowerment is not something that can be done to people; it has to be done by them and is therefore closely associated with the idea of partnership.'

(Thompson, 2011, p. 85)

In some cases, this may mean communities creating their own power through self-help and independent action. In other cases, a more campaigning stance could be taken, which will involve people being in conflict with authorities, public bodies or private companies. These options, described as 'pathways', are discussed in Chapter 4. Practitioners need to consider their own position on these issues and their understanding of the term 'community empowerment' in order to be consistent and effective in their work with communities.

'Empowerment is about working with people and groups to release their potential. I believe, whilst we cannot empower people directly, we can only help people discover their own empowerment.'

(Community Worker, Leeds)

Notes: The four main themes for strengthening communities

The approach to strengthening communities used in this book is based on four key themes:

- Building Organisations
- Building People
- Building Involvement
- Building Equality

The four themes were originally developed by Barr and Hashagen (Barr and Hashagen, 2000). Originally called 'Community empowerment dimensions', they were described in process and outcome terms as follows:

- Personal empowerment: a learning community
- Positive action: a fair and just community
- Community organisation: an active community
- Participation and involvement: an influential community

This useful model was called 'Achieving Better Community Development' or ABCD. Confusingly the same set of initials were unfortunately later used by other writers later to refer to Asset Based Community Development! The model also proposed that through community empowerment, communities could then usually engage in some sort of partnership with public services or others to promote the following set of 'quality of community life' dimensions:

- a shared wealth: community economic development
- a caring community: social and service development
- a safe and healthy community: community environmental action
- a creative community: arts and cultural development
- a citizens' community: governance and development.

Overarching all this was the notion of a 'healthy community' that is liveable, equitable and sustainable. The framework was later developed further by Changes Consultancy for the Community Exchange network. A practical assessment toolkit was produced through a research project in Bradford (Skinner and Wilson, 2002). The framework has been used widely across the UK, and the Scottish Community Development Centre published a toolkit based on the framework called *Building Stronger Communities* (The Scottish Community Development Centre, 2012). In this publication, the four themes have been updated to address the current social and economic context.

Summary of main points

Chapter 1 has introduced some key material including:

> A brief description of the current economic and social climate

> A working definition of the term 'strong communities', with seven key features

> Different ways to understand the terms 'community' and 'communities'

> Insights into the meaning of the term 'community empowerment'.

Points have been the following:

> The current economic climate presents serious challenges to traditional levels of service provision and has created increased pressures on communities.

> Strengthening communities is also about enhancing community empowerment.

> Community empowerment is part of the process of strengthening communities, but not presented here as an end in its own right.

> Practitioners need to consider the role of *power* in communities – this theme is returned to in Chapter 4.

> That empowerment cannot be given, but practitioners can support communities to discover, fight for and win their own empowerment.

The chapter started with a definition of the term 'strong communities'. This book focuses on the first three of the seven key features given in that definition: *active, organised* and *participative*. As mentioned, this is because the author's experience is mostly in these areas and because to address all seven features would need at least two publications! The book draws on community development approaches, but places these in the current climate and the context of building stronger communities.

The material in Chapter 1 is an introduction to some of the issues around community empowerment and building strong communities. In practice, strengthening communities means working in a range of ways in communities: supporting and challenging *individuals* as discussed in Chapter 2; developing community *groups,* as examined in Chapter 3; using and comparing *pathways*, as explored in Chapter 4; building *networks* as briefly discussed in Chapter 5; and *partnership* working at strategic level as reviewed in the last part of the book, Chapter 6.

Notes

This definition of 'strong communities' with the seven key features was devised by the author, based on work over several years with residents' groups, community of interest groups, community leaders and public services around the UK. It is still a working definition, rather than set in stone; it can be developed further through research and the experience of using it. The seven features of strong communities require research to examine such questions as: Do poorer areas display fewer of the seven features? Once strongly present, how can the features be maintained? Do areas with more transient populations make it more difficult for the seven features to be achieved and maintained? How do the seven features contribute to higher levels of social capital? How can the seven features be measured, and their impact be assessed?

Developing your practice

Questions that you as a student, practitioner or policy-maker may wish to consider include the following:

➤ What does the definition of 'strong communities', with seven key features, mean to you? Do the features describe what you believe in?

➤ If in the UK, how has the recent environment of austerity affected you and the communities you work with?

➤ What examples can you think of that you perceive as describing community empowerment?

➤ What does 'community empowerment' mean to you personally? When have you felt empowered in your life?

➤ What is preventing you from feeling more empowered?

➤ What is preventing communities you work with from being more empowered?

➤ What values will underlie your work as a community practitioner?

Box 1.4 What does capacity building mean?

Capacity building is a part of the support needed to strengthen communities. It can be defined as:

'A process of learning and change that increases the ability of individuals and organisations to contribute to the development of communities.'

(Skinner, 2006)

▶

◀

However, it is useful to identify two different versions within this general definition:

Community capacity building means activities, resources and support that strengthen the skills, abilities and confidence of people and groups to take effective action and leading roles in the development of communities.

Agency capacity building is learning, resources and organisational change that increase the ability of public sector and larger voluntary organisations organisations to engage with communities effectively.

In other words, it is useful to highlight that there are different types of capacity building. The term 'agency capacity building' is useful, because it recognises that public and private sector organisations need to enhance their own abilities to engage effectively with and strengthen communities. This is explored in Chapter 6.

More broadly, the term 'capacity building' has also been associated with focusing on gaps in individual or organisational abilities, rather than the approach taken in this publication, which is to value the assets, skills and strengths already existing in communities.

In this publication, the term *community capacity building* (CCB) is used to refer to specific programmes of support, such as a training course organised for community leaders, or grant schemes designed to fund the growth and development of local groups. One concern is that the term can be patronising in tone, in contrast to a partnership approach to CCB, where all interested parties are involved in development and change.

While it is not now a widely used term in England, in Scotland CCB is one of the three main government-led community learning and development (CLD) priorities. Within CLD, CCB sits alongside youth work and adult learning, and is a recognised profession for the CLD and voluntary sector workforce.

Box 1.5 The Big Local approach

Big Local is a programme of support for areas across England, where each area has been awarded just over £1 million of Lottery funding as a grant to be spent over a 10-year period. Several examples used later in this book come from Big Local areas, so the approach is introduced here. The scheme was established by what was originally called the Big Lottery Board, arising from concerns that some areas of England had not fully benefited from a fair share of funding. In total, 150 areas have now received the award, with areas being defined in each case through consultation with the local authority and voluntary sector organisations. For areas to access the award, each needed a partnership of residents to be in place, either building on an existing one or, as in most cases, newly created. The programme is now well-established with many local partnerships halfway through their 10-year funding period. The Big Local

▶

◄

programme is refreshingly different from past regeneration schemes, such as the Single Regeneration Budget, which were often dominated by professionals and politicians making decisions on behalf of the local community. Obviously, in the current climate, having access to a significant funding source is an unusual setting, but Big Local has demonstrated the effectiveness of giving local residents the leading role in initiatives to improve the area and enhance community capacity.

Across England, Big Local partnerships have invested in a wide variety of schemes, from small-scale grants for community activities to larger capital investments to improve local facilities. Projects have included funding employment schemes, housing and park development projects, arts events and festivals. A key feature of the Big Local programme is that local partnerships are led by residents from the area, rather than by politicians and professionals. In practice, this has meant many people getting involved in working together and making decisions about local grants and projects, in some cases with little prior experience of managing public monies.

Big Local partnerships take different forms depending on local preferences – from a defined committee or 'Big Local Board' to more open-ended networks. Whatever form partnerships take, a condition on accessing the award is that the partnership connects with and involves a broad range of people from the area. Each partnership needs to draw up a Big Local Plan, describing how the award can be directed to building strengths and addressing needs in the area. Crucially, this plan is drawn up by the resident-led partnership, though help from professionals has often been used.

Most partnerships have active support from public services and voluntary organisations operating in the Big Local area, who contribute staff time and resources to increase the impact of the Big Local initiative. Each partnership also uses a 'Local Trusted Organisation' to administer the finances on their behalf, such as a locally based voluntary organisation. Even with a range of voluntary and public organisations involved, the consistent, underlying feature is one of residents being in control.

References: Chapter 1

Alston, P. (2018) *Statement on Visit to the United Kingdom*. Office of the High Commissioner, Geneva: United Nations.

Anderson, B. (1983) *Imagined Communities; Reflections on the Origin and Spread of Nationalism*. London: Verso.

Audit Scotland (2019) Principles for community empowerment Edinburgh: Audit Scotland

Back, K. and Back, K. (2005) *Assertiveness at Work: A Practical Guide to Handling Awkward Situations*. New York: McGraw-Hill.

Barr, A. and Hashagen, S. (2000) *Achieving Better Community Development, the ABCD Handbook: A Framework for Evaluating Community Development*. London: Community Development Foundation.

Berner, E. and Philips, B. (2008) *Left to Their Own Devices? Community Self Help between Alternative Development and Neo-Liberalism* in Craig, G., Popple, K. and Shaw, M. (eds) *Community Development in Theory and Practice*. Nottingham: Spokesman.

Boudier, P. (1984) *Distinction: A Social Critique of the Judgement of Taste*. London: Routledge.

Butcher, H. (1993) *Introduction* in Butcher, H., Glen, A., Henderson, P. and Smith, J. (eds) *Community and Public Policy*. London: Pluto Press.

Constantino-David, K. (1995) *Community Organising in the Philippines* in Craig, G. and Mayo, M. (eds) *Community Empowerment A Reader in Participation and Development*. London and New Jersey: Zed Books.

Craig, G. and Mayo, M. (1995) *Community Empowerment A Reader in Participation and Development*. London: Zed Books.

Eade, D. and Williams, B. (1995) *The Oxfam Handbook of Development and Relief. Volume*. Oxford: Oxfam.

Farrar, M. (2002) *The Struggle for "Community" in a British Multi-Ethnic Inner City Area – Paradise in the Making*. New York and Lampeter: Edwin Mellen Press.

Fitzpatrick, S., Bramley, G., Filip Sosenko, F., Blenkinsopp, J., Wood, J., Johnsen, S., Littlewood, M. and Watts, B. (2018) *Destitution in the UK 2018*. York: Joseph Rowntree Foundation.

Foley, M. and Edwards, R. (1999) *The Paradox of Civil Society*. Journal of Democracy, 7 (3).

Freire, P. (1972) *The Pedagogy of the Oppressed*. Harmondsworth: Penguin.

Halpern, D. (2005) *Social Capital*. Cambridge: Polity Press.

Harris, K. and McCabe, A. (2017) *Community Action and Social Media: Trouble in Utopia?* Briefing Paper 140. Birmingham: Third Sector Research Centre.

Hay, S. (2008) *Developing Active Networks in Local Communities: A Review of Local Links, A Pilot Programme in West Yorkshire*. York: Joseph Rowntree Foundation.

Hillery, G. (1955) *Definitions of Community Rural Sociology* Volume 20. New Orleans: The Rural Sociological Society.

HM Government (2018) *Civil Society Strategy: Building a Future that Works for Everyone – Executive Summary*. London: HM Government.

Hudson, M., Phillips, J., Ray, K. and Barnes, H. (2007) *Social Cohesion in Diverse Communities*. York: Joseph Rowntree Foundation.

Jones, H., Gunaratnam, Y., Bhattacharyya, G., Davies, W., Dhaliwal, S., Forkert, K., Jackson, E. and Saltus, R. (2017) *Go Home? the Politics of Immigration Controversies*. Manchester: Manchester University Press.

Knight, B. (2015) *The Society We Want*. London: The Alliance Publishing Trust.

Kretzmann, J.P. and McKnight, J.L. (1993) *Building Communities from the Inside Out: A Path Toward Finding and Mobilizing a Community's Assets*. Evanston, IL: Institute for Policy Research.

Ledwith, M. (2011) *Community Development A Critical Approach*. Bristol: Policy Press.

Local Government Information Unit (2018) *The End to Austerity for the Public Services?*. London: LGIU Briefing Note. www.localtrust.org.uk/library/research-and-evaluation/the-future-for-communities.

Locality (2017) *People Power: Findings from the Commission on the Future of Localism*. London

MacDonald, R., Shildrick, T., Webster, C. and Simpson, D. (2005) *Growing up in poor neighbourhoods: The significance of class and place in the extended transitions of 'socially excluded' young adults.* Sociology. 39 (5).

McArdle, J. (1989) *Community Development Tools of the Trade* in Craig, G. and Mayo, M. (eds) 1995 *Community Empowerment A Reader in Participation and Development.* London: Zed Books.

Miller, S.M., Rein, M. and Levitt, P. (1995) *Community Action in the United States* in Craig, G. and Mayo, M. (eds) *Community Empowerment A Reader in Participation and Development.* London and New Jersey: Zed Books.

Ministry of Housing, Communities and Local Government, (2019) By Deeds and their Results: How we will strengthen our communities and nation London: Ministry of Housing, Communities and Local Government

Pugh, A. (2003) *Reaching Out to Your Community.* Bradford: City of Bradford M.D.C.

Putman, R. (2000) *Bowling Alone.* New York: Simon and Schuster Paperbacks.

Ramcharan, P., Gwyneth, R., Grant, G. and Borland, J. (1997) *Empowerment in Everyday Life.* London: Jessica Kingsley Publishers.

The Scottish Community Development Centre (2012) *Building Stronger Communities: A Practical Assessment and Planning Tool for Community Capacity Building in Scotland.* Glasgow: SCDC.

The Scottish Government (2009).

Thompson, N. (2011) *Promoting Equality.* London: Red Globe Press.

Scottish Government *Empowerment Action Plan: Celebrating Success: Inspiring Change.* www.scotland.gov.uk

Select Committee on Charities (2017) *Stronger Charities for a Stronger Society 2017.* London: House of Lords.

Shaw, M. and Mayo, M. (2016) *Class, Inequality and Community Development.* Bristol: Policy Press.

Skinner, S. (2006) *Strengthening Communities.* London: Community Development Foundation.

Skinner, S. and Wilson, M. (2002) *Assessing Community Strengths.* London: The Community Development Foundation.

Somerville, P. (2011) *Understanding Community Politics, Policy and Practice.* Bristol: Policy Press.

Taylor, M. (2003) *Public Policy in the Community.* London: Red Globe Press.

Wales Council for Voluntary Action (2017) *The Goals of the Well-Being of Future Generations (Wales) Act 2015.* Cardiff: WCVA.

Walker, A. (2015) *Resilience in Practice.* London: Local Government Information Unit.

Yeung, R. (2011) *Confidence: The Power to Take Control and Live the Life You Want.* Harlow: Pearson.

Young, I.M. (1990) *Justice and the Politics of Difference.* Princeton, NJ: Polity Press.

2

Building People

Building people is about developing skills, experience, abilities, ways of working and confidence of individuals so that they are able to take active and leading roles in their communities. Community-based learning and development will, for some people, also increase other life opportunities, such as gaining skills for paid work, but the focus here is on learning for community action and engagement. In order for the process of *building people* to be an empowering experience, such support needs to be based on people's own interest in their learning and development, rather than having it imposed on them. In Part One of this chapter, different ways in which people learn and develop in community settings are explored, focusing on members of community groups. Part Two looks at community leadership and how it can be more effective.

Building skills, knowledge and confidence at the grass roots is an important part of strengthening communities. However, the approach here is not based on the assumption that only communities need to enhance their capacity – equally, staff and managers in public sector organisations need to look at how they engage with and support the grass roots, a theme that is looked at in Chapter 5.

Individual involvement

Potentially, a wide range of people with different roles and backgrounds could be involved in community learning activities, and examples of such participants are given in Box 2.1. Practitioners will need to prioritise who they work with from this wide range of possibilities. This could be a difficult decision, especially in the current climate where there are increased pressures on resources, and where practitioners' work priorities may be dictated by the organisation they are based in. Potentially people operating in all of these different roles in communities could be involved in learning and development, but, for the sake of brevity, this chapter focuses on the learning and development of members of community groups and community leaders.

Box 2.1 Potential participants in community learning activities

- Residents who live in the area, village, town or neighbourhood
- Community group members, for example, members of an older person's club, disability group or sports club
- Group leaders, for example, the chairperson of a local club
- Management committee members, for example, members of a community centre
- Volunteers, for example, people who help their neighbours or who help out through a volunteer bureau
- Users of local services
- School governors
- People who share a concern, such as improving the environment
- Faith leaders and members of a church, mosque, synagogue or temple
- Members of an online network interested in their community
- Staff and trustees from voluntary organisations and charities
- Members of a particular cultural group, for example, Polish people
- A 'community representative' from a network of groups, such as a network made up of a number of disability groups
- Elected members of county, borough or district-based local authorities
- Elected members of town and parish councils.

Part One: Members of community groups

When people join a community group, they may become interested in developing their skills and abilities to be more effective as group members. Equally, the group itself may realise it needs to develop new skills and abilities. The learning needs of a group and the individuals within the group will vary depending on a number of factors, such as the *type of group* – for example, a self-help support group would have different learning needs from a committee running a large community centre. Equally, learning needs will be affected by the *aims of the group.* For instance, a group that has just developed a set of ambitious aims may have new, possibly demanding learning needs. Also, the background of the members will influence the level of learning needed – a group of experienced campaigners may already possess particular organisational skills. There are no set stages that groups go through, with different learning needs at different points. For example, a newly formed group may want to develop basic chairing skills, but equally, a well-established group, with a track record of running many different projects, may need to refresh their understanding of more formal chairing methods.

Box 2.2 Skills for group members

Examples of skills, knowledge and abilities often needed by members of community groups:

- Understanding how meetings and committees work
- Knowing how to support volunteers
- Understanding the management of finances and buildings
- Understanding community consultation
- Knowing how the Council works
- Understanding how groups plan activities
- Having awareness of what equal opportunities mean in communities
- Having skills in fund-raising through organising local activities
- Knowing how to run effective campaigns
- Being aware of diversity and inclusion issues
- Having publicity and public speaking skills
- Knowing how to review activities to make them more effective.

For short-hand, the single term *abilities* is now used in this book to describe the skills, abilities, knowledge, ways of working and talents people have and use as group members.

In the current climate as described in Chapter 1, there is a shift of focus in the abilities needed for community action (Burns, 2011), and additional skills and abilities are having to be added to the above list. For example, many groups are increasingly interested in skills associated with community enterprises: how to prepare tenders to run local services, handle an asset transfer, manage staff and generate income from managing buildings. They are also increasingly using social media to communicate and organise campaigns. Taking a stand against cut-backs has become increasingly important as communities face reductions in services and support. Given the increased tensions and divisions described in Chapter 1, addressing equal opportunities, diversity and inclusion is all the more urgent. In some cases, these abilities were being used earlier, but for many groups there is now a shift of emphasis in the current climate.

Starting from strengths

How can community-based learning be an empowering experience? When *building people,* a useful place to start is by ensuring existing abilities are acknowledged and being used well, and this approach is a key part of asset-based community development. Many people have hidden talents that can be useful to a group or the local community but remain unrecognised and underused. Some people are shy about revealing their existing abilities, but with the right support and opportunity can enjoy using them and shine in confidence. Box 2.3 describes practical methods to help people in community groups to appreciate their existing abilities.

Box 2.3 Ways to help groups appreciate their existing abilities

- Hold a review session that includes charting the group's achievements of the last few years, and, against each achievement, note the particular abilities the group used.

- Invite everyone to jot down on a piece of paper a hidden talent, skill or interest which the rest of the group does not know about. Then put all the pieces of paper into a hat and ask group members to take turns to read them out anonymously, with a guessing game on who wrote each one.

- Ask people about their roles in life outside the group, such as running a house, organising play groups, shopping on a tight budget or helping out at the temple or church. These informal roles will often reveal skills people are already using.

- Ask people to bring or share a photo of when they did something unusual, new or adventurous. This is a simple way just to start talking about hidden talents.

'Appreciative Enquiry' is a useful way to help individuals recognise their skills and abilities. It usually involves four stages: discover, dream, design and deliver. The method was used, for example, by the Bradford District Assembly, a network that links the voluntary and community sectors with the public sector. The aim was to increase the number and range of voices from black and minority ethnic communities (BAME) on the Bradford District Assembly and its Forums. An event was held in 2018 with a high level of participation, unearthing stories on, for example, 'the best of what is'. The Appreciative Enquiry process was very effective and produced a broad-ranging action plan to ensure greater BAME involvement.

Many people have fears about education and learning from their experiences at school. Practitioners will need to use some sensitivity in how learning and development is introduced and discussed. Terms such as 'training' may sound a bit formal – the term 'workshop' often goes down better.

Identifying learning needs

In order to help a group or individual choose the right type of learning with an appropriate range of content, it is useful to identify their learning needs in a systematic way. This could be through working with the whole group or with individuals. There are a range of different approaches, where each approach looks at learning needs from a different perspective. For any of these approaches, the list of abilities given earlier is useful as a menu to help the participants look at their learning needs. Several different approaches are now discussed in turn.

Firstly, learning needs can be unearthed by looking at *tasks*. Identifying the specific tasks involved in different activities and roles that the group has can be useful to show specific areas of learning needed. Starting with a forthcoming project, such as a community festival, can make the process clearer. Organising a festival will produce a long list of tasks and may well place new demands on a group. Each task and its associated abilities can be listed, and jobs allocated, with support and learning opportunities identified in each case.

A second approach is to use *plans*. If the group has an action plan or strategy for the next few years, the practitioner can facilitate discussion on what different parts of the plan will mean in terms of abilities needed. This can involve inviting ideas on any gaps that exist in the group's abilities that will need addressing.

Equally, if a group is facing a particular *problem* or process of change, this can be a learning opportunity. For example, taking on a new building through asset transfer will create new demands. While it may cause stress and fears, it could also be used to look at new learning needs. A practitioner can work with the group to identify more clearly new demands that will arise and how these can be addressed through learning activities.

Another approach is to look at different *roles* within the group and how these will generate needs for different skills and abilities. These roles may arise from formal positions, such as chairperson, secretary or treasurer, or from more informal leadership roles within the group, as discussed below. Each role will have a matching set of abilities; a useful place to start is to ask each existing role holder what abilities they think are needed, building on their own experience.

So far, we have briefly looked at *tasks, plans, problems* and *roles* as different approaches to identifying individual learning needs. Three other approaches are:

➤ *Start with the person*. This means getting to know a person as an individual, helping them share what their concerns are, identifying what their existing skills and abilities are and what interests them for future community action. This interest becomes the basis of building their abilities, matching projects and activities to their particular needs and personal motivation. In terms of diversity issues, it is a useful way of involving marginalised people and appreciating their particular backgrounds. This approach is used in youth work in the UK, looking at the longer-term development of the individual. It needs to be a tailor-made approach, and while it is very effective in motivating people, it can be very time consuming. It can also be group based, as part of ongoing meetings, and integrated into a culture of learning and change.

➤ *Start with the organisation*. Instead of focusing on the individual, this approach to identifying learning needs concentrates on the needs of the whole group and the particular challenges and changes it is going through. Chapter 3 explores a range of such challenges, using key questions as a facilitation method to help groups to move forward and achieve their aims. Groups may be working on very different issues; one may be concerned with diversity and expanding its membership, while another may be interested in more effective evaluations. In both of these examples, different learning needs will arise, such as enhanced understanding of diversity in the community and of effective evaluation methods. Consequently, focusing on the organisation and its current concerns, as discussed in Chapter 3, is a useful way to identify learning needs.

➤ *Start with the pathway*. The Wheel of Participation, explored in Chapter 4, can help to look at what are called spokes or *pathways*. *Having a Say*, one of the 'spokes' on the Wheel, could encourage participants to be more assertive and better able to express their views at meetings. *Self-help* could mean the group needs to learn more about team work and how to delegate and share tasks. *Organising for change* could mean the group needs to enhance its abilities to plan and run campaigns.

In practice, identifying learning needs with groups may not be as organised as described so far! Having such a wide range of alternatives may feel overwhelming. Practitioners can try out different approaches where it will benefit, rather than harm, the group. In practice, different approaches can be combined in different ways – a session focusing on a future plan may end up looking at pathways and so on. Another problem is that the person describing their own learning needs may not be aware that they need to enhance their skills in a particular area! For instance, a group has a chairperson who is not very effective at chairing meetings but who is completely unaware of this. Some careful one-to-one discussion could help the person to look at their development needs. A key issue, as mentioned, is to build on and value existing skills, knowledge and experience, thus helping to make the development of abilities an empowering experience.

Box 2.4 Using questionnaires

A questionnaire survey can be used for many of the approaches just described. Such questionnaires usually include a list of skills, abilities, and knowledge areas against which individuals indicate their strengths. This is a widely used method for identifying learning needs. However, the difficulty is to find a list of abilities that is relevant for community groups, as many published lists come from other settings, such as the private sector. A useful resource from public sector is written by O'Hara et al. (2016). One useful way to divide the questions up is by using a set of headings such as:

- *Skills base* – for example, committee skills or publicity skills.

- *Knowledge base* – for example, knowledge of funding sources, how the council works or what valuing diversity means.

- *Understanding* – of the voluntary and community sectors; diversity, inclusion and equal opportunities; community empowerment.

- *Qualities* – such as a can-do attitude or having a problem-solving approach, a commitment to equal opportunities and community empowerment.

The main thing is to keep it accessible in style; if abilities are presented in a way that appears too complex, people will feel alienated. For each ability listed, the participant can be invited to respond under the following headings:

- My strengths

- Areas I am confident in

- My gaps – None, Some, A Lot

- Skills and experience I could share

- Subjects I would like to learn more about

- The type of help I would prefer, such as training or mentoring.

Such terms are not very precise; no doubt, the set of abilities could be described with more precision, for example, using the concept of competencies (Whiddett and Hollyforde, 2003). However, more precise or technical sounding wording on survey forms can be off-putting for some people; keeping to clear and accessible language is helpful.

Box 2.5 Heart, head and hands

An enjoyable way to help members of groups to think about skills needed for community action and leadership is to draw an image of a human body on a flip chart. Then add the headings:

- Head – written on the head
- Heart – written where the heart is
- Hands – written on each hand.

Then invite group members to write in each of the three areas of the body different skills, such as:

Head – knowledge of how committees work

Heart – people skills, handing conflict

Hands – computer skills, practical publicity skills.

(Adapted from a method used at the Big Local Connects event, 2018)

Forms of learning

A knee-jerk reaction to discovering a learning need can be to direct someone to a training course or just hand out leaflets at a meeting and ask if anyone is interested. In practice, a range of different *forms of learning* for community settings is available, each one having different advantages and disadvantages. There is a wealth of experience of community-based learning across the UK to draw on, and this is especially the case in Scotland, which has a long history of community education that addresses the needs of community development.

Different structured forms of learning for community groups to consider and use are now discussed in turn.

Group-based training is where the learning materials are designed for the particular group and where training sessions are held in the group's own centre or in a location, without members of other groups attending. Because it occurs locally in familiar territory and is tailor made, group-based training may increase the level of attendance from within the group. However, because it is limited to the group's own members, participants miss the opportunity to meet members of other groups. Also because it is a tailor-made course or session, it will not be accredited. Even so, a certificate of attendance may be useful for participants.

In contrast, *course-based training* is where the training is held in a central location with members from several groups attending. The content can still be tailor made, based on a training needs review of potential participants, or it can be chosen from established, accredited programmes. The disadvantage of this approach is that, if it is a pre-set course, some of the content may not interest everyone and a central location may put off some people from attending.

In contrast to training, *mentoring* normally involves one-to-one support between two people, where one person provides advice and guidance based on their more extensive skills and experience. In Leeds, for example, the director of a voluntary organisation received one-to-one mentoring over a six-month period from the author during a time of transition and change. The sessions explored the pros and cons of different options that the director's organisation faced, including a merger with a much larger organisation. As a method, *mentoring* can provide more individual encouragement and support than, say, *course-based training*. Also the mentor themselves may be a useful role model, though often the mentor learns a lot from the mentee. In practice, while high in impact, informal mentoring schemes in community settings are demanding to set up to ensure effective matches of mentor and mentee.

Reviews can be very useful, for example where, after events and activities have been organised by a community group, a review session is held, dedicated to learning from the experience. Useful questions are: What went well? What did not go so well? How can we do a better job next time? Such a review session could also be part of a larger-scale evaluation of the organisation's future direction and plans, for example, during an away-day. The chairperson of a community group in Leeds made notes after each event the group had organised and at the next meeting encouraged discussion on both what went well and how they could do an even better job next time. Such review sessions can have positive impact, as long as participants are open to reflection and the feedback is handled with some sensitivity. Equally, some group members may be defensive and not open to hearing feedback, in which case other methods may be more appropriate.

Another learning method is through arranging *visits*; for example, a group wanting to set up a new community enterprise visits one already working well. Groups learn directly from each other and such visits can be a morale boost – 'we could do the same!'. An Asian women's group in Halifax used a first ever trip to London to develop ideas for a community enterprise. To be effective, such visits need to be carefully arranged and facilitated, with the host group aware of what the visiting group needs. At worst it can become a showcase marketing opportunity for the host group, with little critical reflection. A community group in Salford visited a well-established community education centre to get ideas for their own estate. The visit sparked a review of what they wanted, both with some similarities and some important differences from the one they visited. Visits were also used as part of the 'Together We Are Bradford' cohesion initiative in 2017/18 (Anderton, 2018). This government-funded programme aimed to build relationships and better understanding between different cultures. Visits to different centres were valuable for the group to get away from their own locality and experience a new place together. The report states that visits helped people learn about how things operate in different communities and to consider their own situation more objectively.

The discussion so far has shown the rich diversity of forms of learning that exist and that each one will have different advantages and disadvantages. Box 2.6 gives a few ideas on social media and the internet as a learning arena, and Box 2.7 provides a round-up of several other forms of learning.

Box 2.6 Social media and the internet

Social media have great potential as a learning medium. For example, *webinars* are online conferences, facilitated by a lead person who invites a speaker based in a different location to talk on a theme. People watching online type questions and comments, with immediate responses from the speaker after the talk. Webinars can offer cheap ways to get decision-makers and high-profile figures into the homes of people who would never attend a public meeting. They can be recorded and played again to audiences that missed them or be streamed online for additional viewings. Publicity is needed to spread the word and encourage sign-on for the webinar at the time it is to be aired. While webinars are still underused as a community learning tool, they can be very effective, but do require certain equipment.

Blogging can help create a personal diary or journal for an ongoing project or campaign. Blogging is relatively easy and can create a sense of community, reaching a large audience simultaneously. It is mainly used via a programme called Wordpress, which offers hundreds of free designs and layouts. Creating and responding to blogs is an interesting learning method. However, the disadvantages of blogging include the need for the blog to be updated regularly, and problems can occur around controversial discussions and strong differences of opinion. Blogging can also encourage large amounts of 'trolling', that is, unwanted, irrelevant or offensive comments, although free software is available that can address this.

Online courses are where individuals follow a structured learning programme online, designed by an educational institution. A wide range of these is available, with varying degrees of online support. One problem can be that the participant may feel isolated and miss a group learning experience. A useful new initiative in this field is called MOOCs – Mass Online Open Courses.

Box 2.7 More forms of learning in community settings

Other forms of learning used in community settings are *on-the-job coaching*. For example, a deputy chairperson who does not have much chairing experience might chair meetings and then get feedback from the existing chairperson after each meeting.

Awareness-raising sessions can be very effective, where a group explores a particular theme with a facilitator, such as disability issues or racism. Such sessions can be turning points in people's awareness but need to be facilitated with care in order to to involve and challenge people rather than just alienate them. A bit old fashioned but still very useful is to bring in *visiting speakers* to the group. Outside speakers can be invited to discuss their views and experience on a current local issue or to present a proposal. A key need is to brief the speaker so that they have some idea of the group's background prior to giving the talk.

Peer groups are an opportunity for people in similar positions such as chairs of community groups to get together on a regular basis to share issues and ideas. UnLtd, a national charity supporting social enterprise, uses peer networks as a form of learning to support local people involved in starting their own social businesses.

Action learning is where a closed group is formed that meets regularly over several months in a central location. Individual members take turns during sessions to share a challenge or problem. In action learning, the method is usually that the other group members primarily ask questions in response to the problem in order to encourage reflection about their challenge or problem, rather than immediately attempt to problem-solve or give advice. In further sessions, members then share progress on follow-up actions taken since the last session.

Briefing sessions is where a group of community activists or representatives is given an update on a situation in advance of an important meeting or event. It could be used, for example, prior to a key meeting between residents and council officers, where the community group members are given an outline of issues involved. This method was used to good effect in the Bradford New Deal for Communities programme.

Shadowing is an interesting learning method, where, for example, a new community representative sits with a more experienced community representative to observe them in action at several networking meetings. This could involve, for instance, a community leader in effect following a senior officer in a public sector organisation over two days in order to see them in action and understand how their organisation operated.

Games and simulations have great potential to engage learners and create exciting dynamics that enrich learning. For example, simulations with role-plays of meetings can be run between community representatives and public service managers. While they can be very effective, a key issue is to choose the appropriate game or simulation that will engage rather than alienate the participants.

Guided reading is where individuals are invited to follow a suggested reading list on a particular subject. Publications can be accessed through loans, subsidised purchases or in some cases, free online. Follow-up discussion sessions with a learning facilitator can be an opportunity to share views on the material.

In general, a consideration is that the participants in any learning method and whatever level of ability feel supported by the experience, rather than suffer a loss of confidence. For some people, being invited to get involved in anything that sounds like school may produce strong reactions. This may especially be the case where people may have long held fears about education, are not using their mother tongue and are not confident about reading and writing. So, building trust over time is crucial to enable involvement. It is inspiring how people start low in self-confidence and, over time, blossom through gaining new skills and making better use of their existing personal strengths. Some group members may become interested in moving on to related further or higher education courses, such as community development, social work, project management, leadership studies or youth work. A community activist on an estate in Bradford said:

> 'I left school when I was fourteen and now they want me to run the community centre!'

She later became the chairperson of the centre's committee and then, after five years, became a city-wide representative of tenants' associations. Through different roles over several years, she built her own confidence and recognised the value of her prior experience as an activist. Such changes can be seen as a journey of building confidence and sense of self-worth over time.

Stages of learning

Having a variety of *forms of learning* available to use with group members is important, because research has indicated that adults learn in different ways. Kolb contributed some important insights into understanding how people learn as a problem-solving experience with four stages (Kolb, 1984). In the context of strengthening communities, this could be from *concrete experiences,* such as a community group organising a local consultation meeting or from *reflection*, where the experience is interpreted, questioned and meaning explored, through using questions such as: How did the meeting go? What went well? What did it mean to them? Another key stage is called *conceptualisation*, where the experience is examined in the light of beliefs, attitudes or theories. In this case, the consultation meeting could be considered by looking at the Ladder of Participation discussed later in Resource Five. There is also a stage of *experimentation*, where the insights gained from the first three stages are applied in practice. In this case, another consultation meeting could be organised, avoiding some of the problems encountered in the first one.

Kolb suggested the cycle repeats, where the experimentation of one cycle becomes the basis of the next cycle. In practice, learning will often not be a set of neat sequential stages, but the stages could occur in a different order. Kolb's model is helpful to point out that people learn in different ways – having a range of forms of learning available to groups means they can choose ones based on their strengths.

Over time, individual learners may need support to broaden their abilities; for example, some people may be strong on reflection but not then apply their learning in the real world. Facilitators can help groups and individuals look at their learning strengths and identify weaker areas. For example, the author worked with a community group over a year helping them develop action plans for new projects, but in practice the plans did not get implemented. Obviously, such occurrences can be due to a number of factors, but Kolb's framework is useful to highlight where blocks and barriers may be occurring.

Kolb's work led to the idea that adults have different learning styles, and Honey and Mumford then developed a learning styles questionnaire (Honey and Mumford, 1982).

Box 2.8 The influence of Freire

Leading Brazilian educationalist Paulo Freire was a major figure in the educational arena in the late twentieth century with his theory of liberating education, viewing literacy as a weapon for social change. In his approach, providing education to individuals oppressed within society is seen as a way of breaking away from the 'culture of silence' and transforming the world around them (Ali, 2018). Although his work was conducted over 50 years ago, it continues to retain its political and pedagogical pertinence to 'emancipate the oppressed' and contribute to social transformation (Ireland, 2018).

In his book *Pedagogy of the Oppressed*, Freire begins by explaining the central problem for mankind as 'humanisation'. Although all individuals have a desire for humanisation, this desire is constantly denied and justified by the 'oppressors', leading to dehumanisation (Freire, 1996). This dehumanising experience, however, is a direct consequence of the power imbalances existing in society (Freire, 1996) with economic disparities as a leading factor (Ledwith, 2016). High levels of poverty are seen to create a sense of powerlessness, robbing people of their hopes and aspirations, so that they feel dehumanised (Ledwith, 2016). For the oppressed to recover their lost humanity, they need to become restorers of humanity by weakening the power of the oppressors and highlighting the injustices and exploitation faced by the oppressed (Freire, 1996). Through intertwining practice and knowledge together in one process, critical consciousness is nurtured (Ledwith, 2016).

Barriers to effective learning

Members of community groups may experience a number of barriers that reduce their level of participation in learning opportunities. This could be lack of confidence or fears about education from school days. Unfortunately, some potential participants may not feel welcome, either because of the communication style of the people running the sessions or because learning groups seem dominated by people of a certain background. For some people, lack of language, numeracy or literacy skills or the costs involved can be off-putting, and venues may be inaccessible or hard to get to. More fundamentally, the learning opportunities may not match people's needs, so they do not feel motivated. Practitioners can work with groups to identify what such barriers are. This work requires some flexibility as it is likely that these barriers will vary between groups and also vary between individuals within any one group. Barriers to participation are also looked at in Chapter 5.

Box 2.9 Content of learning programmes for strengthening communities

As well as choosing the appropriate *forms of learning*, the *content* of the learning will obviously be central to *building people*. As indicated above, ideally the content is tailor made, based on a systematic process of identifying learning needs. Various options for content are, for example:

- The abilities and skills listed in this chapter in Box 2.2
- Asset-based community development
- Diversity and inclusion
- Effective community engagement
- Project management
- Planning events and activities
- Managing volunteers
- Leadership and community representation
- Community profiles
- Partnerships and the public sector
- Safeguarding and the protection of children and adults at risk
- Power, empowerment and discrimination.

◄

These are just a few examples. To build communities that are stronger, based on the definition given in Chapter 1, learning opportunities will be needed that help individuals and groups explore what building stronger communities means in practice. In addition, content could specifically address the seven features in the definition of strengthening communities and cover issues such as:

- *Active* – What barriers prevent community groups and others from being more involved in local community activities and community action to improve the quality of life?

- *Organised* – What would help communities to come together to form and sustain groups, networks and organisations that address common problems and provide local services?

- *Participative* – How can groups contribute to decisions that affect members' lives and people have a real say about the issues that concern them?

- *Resourceful* – How can members of groups use their abilities to be more enterprising and resourceful?

- *Accepting* – How can people be more accepting of each other in communities, with an understanding of different cultures, traditions and beliefs?

- *Connected* – How can areas build a sense of belonging, where people and groups from different backgrounds and identities have meaningful contact and communication?

- *Fair* – How can communities be developed where people from different backgrounds and identities have a similar level of opportunities and where social injustice and discrimination are actively challenged?

Notes: Community development learning standards

The Endorsement and Quality Standards Board for Community Development Learning (ESB) was set up in 1997 through a series of community development conferences in England called Towards 2001. ESB provides a robust system of endorsement of quality for all types of training and learning in community development. Their role is to ensure quality standards in training and learning for community development practitioners. See: www.esbendorsement.org.uk

Creative approaches to building people

So far, this chapter has focused on structured community-based learning. However, *building people* is much more than just developing abilities; it can equally be seen as a process of supporting people to discover their own empowerment; it is about personal growth and change as much as obtaining new skills and knowledge (Thompson, 2006). The emphasis has mainly been on *learning* rather than a broader process of personal development and empowerment. For example, confidence building can occur through community-based learning, but, equally, confidence can be built through people getting involved in new activities.

Examples of creative ways in which groups and individuals have built their confidence and abilities are given below. These fascinating examples, including arts projects, community research, self-reliant groups and assertiveness training, have been contributed by a range of organsations across the UK and include an interesting example of community organising from the US. They have been included in order to demonstrate more creative and informal methods to support adult learning. Some show the importance of setting, such as the sheds movement; others focus on the use of the arts. These experiences, through using creative and informal approaches to learning, can be just as important, if not more empowering, as more structured forms of learning; an imaginative approach to *building people* is the key.

'Winning the regional award given by Tpas for Tenant of the Year Award was a major boost to my confidence.'

(Community leader, Blackburn)

Carnival arts in Leeds

Community arts have great potential for enhancing awareness and unearthing hidden talents. The Harrison Bundey Mama Dread's Masqueraders are a carnival troupe, performing each August at the West Indian Carnival in Chapeltown, north Leeds. Each year they use preparation for the carnival as a way to explore different social issues (Farrar et al., 2017). They are made up of people from a variety of backgrounds and ages who work together over several months to design costumes for their carnival performance. They have been performing for more than 20 years with over 100 performers and 170 costume makers.

'It is inspiring to be in a collective, to be on the road and perform on the streets, being proud of our own identity'.

(Troupe member, The Bundey Mama Dread's Masqueraders)

Each year the troupe uses a different theme for their design and performance and spends time between costume making discussing the issues involved. The process starts with a review of the last performance and discussion is facilitated by a group member. Themes have included police racism, environmental issues, saving the NHS, migration and the abolition of slavery. The troupe see themselves as storytellers, using satire and visual imagery to explore key issues in a positive way. Members have grown in their awareness of wider social issues through their involvement and have gained in confidence, discovering and building skills and talents.

Community organising in the US

The theory of community organising is about harnessing the power of individuals to work together in their shared self-interest, involving outreach at local level, building relationships, mobilising people and supporting projects which make a real difference. In the UK many different organisations have been involved in community organising in the last few decades, including central government funded programmes. In the US, one form of community organising has involved building local networks to be ready for action when needed; leaders build up their followers through one-to-one interviews to form a web of relationships, though a more team-based approach is often preferred (Schutz and Sandy, 2011). Community organising is mainly about social and political change through collective action. In particular, the approach is based on listening carefully to what people want in their lives and in the community, and helping them to achieve this, working through democratic structures. It is about careful listening to local needs, rather than starting with an agenda of what is needed. Through responding to people's particular interests and needs, community organising also builds confidence and awareness.

Community organising has a long history, including the Zapatista movement in Mexico and the labour movement in the US from the mid-nineteenth century onwards (Schutz and Sandy, 2011; Twelvetrees, 2017).

Men's and women's sheds in Porth, Wales

The Men's and Women's Sheds in South Wales are self-sufficient, self-managed, sustainable community groups. They were initially set up in the Porth area by a community organisation, called ShedNet, in order to address social isolation and loneliness, using a community development approach. ShedNet was established in 2016 specifically to help support the opening of Men's and Women's Sheds across South Wales valley communities. The Cwm Taf Primary Care Cluster has funded the ShedNet project and sheds in other areas since 2016. Sheds have particularly attracted men as a space where they can belong to a unique group, pursue their interests and develop new ones, feel useful and have a sense of belonging.

The idea started in Australia where there are now over 2000 Men's Sheds. The approach soon spread to Ireland with over 200 sheds established. Once set up, they are self-governing with a small committee, their own individual constitution, their own income and eventually their own premises. In order to establish new sheds, ShedNet usually carries out a survey of community groups in the area to involve them in the project and identify local needs.

Activities in sheds vary depending on the skills and interests of the group. While many are wood-working groups, there is also a wide range of other activities on offer. Support includes community development training, recognition of existing skills and help forming a business. 'Shedders' may be artists, collectors, story-tellers, amateur radio enthusiasts, train spotters, and model makers. Anyone is welcome, and any interest, skill or project is given consideration – especially if it could attract new members or gain valuable income to support the development of the entire group.

All sheds are open to men and women, though they have mostly attracted men. ShedNet has also set up the second Women's Shed in Wales, where activities include arts and crafts. Across Wales the programme is expanding, with an additional 50 in the pipeline.

Community-based assertiveness training in Leeds

Assertiveness training is an accessible way for members of communities to build their personal confidence and improve their communication skills. A Leeds-based disability group wanted to be more effective in their campaigning work, so invited the author as a trainer to run an assertiveness training course for their members. The course lasted six months with a session per fortnight and was designed to be down to earth and practical in content. The group went from strength to strength, negotiating with senior managers in the local authority about facilities, and challenging oppressive attitudes in their everyday lives.

Assertiveness training usually includes material on assertive rights and a variety of practical techniques. Assertive rights include beliefs, such as the right to be respected, the right to be heard, and the right to say 'no'. Exploring and owning such rights can be a powerful and liberating experience, especially for people who have been down-trodden in some way in their family, group or community.

An important starting point is the concept that we are all already assertive to some extent, but all need to develop greater assertiveness, whatever our background or status in life. Assertiveness theory states that there are four different types of behaviour – assertive, passive, aggressive and indirectly aggressive. A common mistake is that being assertive is confused with being aggressive, so exploring the four types of behaviour is useful to clarify the difference.

Learning to be more assertive as a group can help to build relationships and create a more effective group culture. The idea of rights is important in

assertiveness training, though, equally important, is the concept of matching responsibilities. For example, matching the right to be respected is the
responsibility to respect others; the right to be heard carries the responsibility
to listen to others. Being assertive is definitely not about dominating or always
winning over others; it is more about building equal, effective relationships,
based on mutual respect.

Community research in Salford

In the Little Hulton Big Local area, Salford, a research team of eight local
people was recruited with a range of experience and qualifications. The only
appointment criteria were passion for the area and a willingness to work outside their comfort zone. The research, over a 10-week period, focused on the
future of a local park, involving conversations with residents, based on questionnaires designed by the researchers. This was complemented by individual
short projects focusing on a particular aspect of the issue under scrutiny.
Researchers were encouraged to organise visits and conduct interviews with
key influencers and decision makers, such as councillors. The learning outcomes of these methods varied with the individual researcher. The research
outcomes reflected a consensus and an aggregation of perspectives informing
choices for the future of the local park.

The learning outcomes for the research team were built around an Open
Learning Level 3 Research Skills module, which expects learners to demonstrate understanding of the need for planning, ethical delivery and objective evaluation. To demonstrate this, researchers were asked to write two
short assignments of up to 1000 words, one on the principles of community
research and one on the findings of an individual or paired piece of research
involving a good cross section of the community.

Learning in this process was a unique experience for each person. Writing a focused assignment was a major task for all researchers and had to
be supported on a one-on-one basis. Those with higher education experience and those with limited formal education needed support in different
ways.

By the end of 10 weeks, based on a commitment of 10 hours per week,
the researchers were 'seeing with new eyes and listening with new ears'
by working as a team, experiencing the stages of group development and
increasing their observational skills. An appreciable common gain for the
researchers was seeing the community in a different and more positive light
and a growth in their own confidence to participate and challenge the status
quo. Providing a range of challenging experiences, which all researchers committed to participating in, was a key to shaping successful outcomes for each
person. Everyone had a chance to shine.

Self-Reliant Groups in Scotland and Wales

This approach was developed in India and Bangladesh, and there are now Self-Reliant Groups (SRGs) in England, Scotland and Wales. An organisation called WEvolution helped to set them up in Scotland, where the initiative grew out of a 10-day immersion trip hosted by the Church of Scotland in 2011 through which women from some of Glasgow's least understood communities experienced at first hand the transformative impact of women's self-help groups in India. The SRG approach nurtures an environment wherein people, especially women, are enabled to come together to help each other, save small amounts of money, learn together and create products or services bringing hope and value to their lives, and in the long term, to their families and local communities.

Now flourishing in several regions of the UK, SRGs are based on the principles of self-help, trust and collective endeavour towards their social and economic well-being. Group members collectively strive towards improving their confidence, reducing their sense of isolation and growing their aspirations to take more control of their lives. Self-reliant groups usually consist of 4–10 people who are from a local community and have a similar background and who want to make differences in their lives. Each group meets regularly, and members agree their own aims and common purposes; but they follow the principles of self-help, supporting each other and working together.

In Wales, following in WEvolution's steps, Purple Shoots has, since 2014, helped to set up ten SRGs. Purple Shoots is a not-for-profit micro-finance organisation, dedicated to tackling unemployment and economic problems. Purple Shoots helps the groups get going and offers help and advice, but once established, the groups run themselves. If the groups develop a business idea which needs a small loan, Purple Shoots can offer the funds for this.

Being involved in an SRG has led to increased self-confidence, friendships and warm connections between individuals, involvement in community activities, role modelling for children and families and enterprising endeavour including a community café, launderette and a high-end arts and crafts store on a high street amongst other micro-enterprises.

Using Freire's approach in Edinburgh

The Adult Learning Project in Edinburgh, affectionately known as ALP, uses the principles of Brazilian educator Paulo Freire in its work, as a part of the wider use of Friere's approaches across Scotland (Kirkland and Kirkland, 2011). Freire's approaches and methods, mentioned earlier, have been used in the centre's learning groups with great effect. Learning groups have included the arts, writing, sport and women's history. The fundamental concern in all of Paulo Freire's philosophy is about challenging the passivity and fatalism of ordinary people, enabling them to help themselves out of what can be called the 'culture of silence'. Through its teaching styles and curriculum, ALP has made an important contribution to enabling marginalised voices of Scottish communities to be heard. For educators the world over who share similar aims and values, the experience of ALP has been insightful and inspirational.

Using Freire's approach in Lancashire

The University of Central Lancashire's Centre for Volunteering and Community Leadership (CVCL) was founded in 1999 and has since won several awards for its extensive work on community cohesion and active citizenship within Lancashire. Through the CVCL's ethos, to engage, empower and enable people to reach their true potential, they have been able to support approximately 17,000 UCLan students. The students have been able to develop their skills by engaging in and leading on innovative projects at both a local and international level. The CVCL's commitment to transformative social change through emancipatory action research has played a major role in achieving this, influenced by the work of Paulo Freire (see Box 2.8). High levels of poverty are seen by Freire to create a sense of powerlessness, robbing people of their hopes and aspirations, in turn feeling dehumanised (Ledwith, 2016). This is apparent in the Northwest of England, where there are several wards experiencing high levels of deprivation, coupled with a vast number of unemployed people. The elements of placements allow the students to apply theory in action and develop theory from the action (Ledwith, 2016). Reflection, however, plays a key role in developing theory from action and this takes shape in the form of dialogue between the tutor and the students. It is the role of the tutor to mediate the action-reflection process and allow the students to come to the critical awareness of their reality (Ledwith, 2011). This shift from naïve consciousness to critical consciousness liberates and empowers the individuals to take the necessary actions to transform their reality.

Projects such as the Global Youth Solution (GYS), offered by the CVCL, provide students with a platform to engage in dialogue and reflect on topical issues affecting their lives and develop methods to overcome these challenges. GYS was developed with the same ethos to engage, empower and enable students in fulfilling their true potential using the teaching methods suggested by Freire. Shifting the power of learning to the student provides them with the opportunity to empower themselves through their own learning. The role of the tutor is to facilitate the sessions in order to ensure learning is taking place; however, the learning must be guided by the students. Posing problems about 'codified existential situations' allows learners to arrive at a more critical view of their reality, supporting them to develop a self-awareness which will free them to be more than just 'passive objects'. This transformative learning method has been rolled out with groups of young people across the Northwest through various training and leadership events. This model has since been adopted in other countries and CVCL are currently working with universities across Oman to embed this into their curriculum.

A citizens' jury in Blackburn

The project, organised by Blackburn Healthy Living, involved working with residents living on the Shadsworth estate in the Shadsworth and Whitebirk ward of Blackburn. A citizens' jury approach was adopted to run the project and ran over a four-month period, which involved recruitment of residents, facilitation of the jury's debates and the production of recommendations and reports. Sixteen residents were involved in the jury, made up of 6 men and 10 women, most of whom had not been involved in any form of community-based programmes previously. They attended weekly sessions, including, after an introduction, five sessions in which commentators were invited to discuss their work, plus two further sessions that were used to consider all the 'evidence' and produce a set of recommendations.

Part of the process of a citizens' jury involved inviting voluntary and public sector service providers as commentators to each of the meetings to present what and how their services were doing in relation to a particular subject matter. This was followed by a series of questions and further discussions and debate between the commentator and the residents. In total, 10 commentators attended the 5 sessions. These included representatives from credit unions, the Citizens' Advice Bureau, the Brian Shields' Trust, housing associations and the local authority. Subjects discussed ranged from illegal money lending to fuel poverty. The citizens' jury process allows citizens to reflect and discuss with each other on the questions at hand, occasionally assisted by a facilitator. They are also given the opportunity to scrutinise the information they receive from each commentator, whom they interrogate themselves. Once the recommendations have been agreed, the members of the jury present them to decision makers, in this case the local authority.

A combined approach in Sandyhills, Glasgow

From July 2017 to May 2018, the Wheatley Group, a housing association based in Glasgow, commissioned the Scottish Community Development Centre (SCDC) to provide community support and development services to a community group based around Sandyhills Community Hall in the east end of Glasgow. Development sessions were held with community volunteers to take stock of progress in Sandyhills, discuss and work through their collective purpose and set outcomes for the development work. In October 2017, the group decided to become a Registered Tenants Organisation with the name Sandyhills Community Organisation. The culmination of this process was Sandyhills Community Organisation's first AGM, held in January 2018. Those elected to the committee were all from the Sandyhills area and none had any previous membership of a management committee. A good balance was reached between men and women and younger and older committee members. Committee members were largely those community volunteers SCDC had previously been working with. This committee and post holders now became the focus of their support. At this point, committee members decided to prioritise committee skills training and capacity for attracting funds. Individuals involved felt they were starting from a very low level of skills, understanding and community connections.

Sessions were held to support the development of skills, particularly around chairing meetings, taking minutes and communicating with the community. Younger community members, themselves trained in committee skills by an organisation called YoMo, were able to cascade that training to other committee members. Development sessions, training and visits held to increase collective capacity to attract funding to Sandyhills Community Organisation included a visit to Glasgow Soup, a crowd-funded public dinner where people meet and vote to make local community-based projects and ideas a reality. This visit furthered links with local community groups, who provided practical development advice around constitutions and the music group. It also involved attendance at funding advice sessions delivered by Glasgow Centre for the Voluntary Sector, covering making a case for grant support, the application process, funding searches using the online tool 'First Funding Stop' and where to go for further information. A visit from representatives of Big Lottery Scotland to Sandyhills helped to build further capacity so as to attract funding through a question and answer session and give a commitment of ongoing support and advice.

Learning journeys

One way to understand how people grow in confidence and levels of empowerment is to see the process as a *learning journey*, which includes a range of key elements and experiences where an individual grows and changes over time. The examples given above demonstrate the many different ways people get involved in their own learning journey. A learning journey may happen in different ways over time, based on a range of challenges and opportunities. For practitioners, it means helping people to recognise how, in their personal and family life and through experiences in groups and campaigns, their skills and abilities will develop and grow over time. This recognition reflects the values of an asset-based community development approach. This type of support can also include encouraging people to plan for time to reflect and think about actions that have been taken and to ask themselves if these could be done differently or better. It means encouraging openness to different ways of learning, including formal activities, for example, training and mentoring, as well as more creative and informal ones.

For practitioners, the approach means seeing the person as a whole person, rather than just a set of needs. A reflective approach is central – taking time to consider what has been learned and how it will be applied in future. Finally, learning journeys are about people's involvement in the design of learning – helping people think about the ways that they learn best and how to celebrate personal achievements.

This chapter has described a range of formal and informal approaches to community-based learning. As shown, *building people* can occur in a wide range of situations and settings and be part of a practitioner's general way of working in communities.

Part Two: Community leaders

So far in this chapter, the focus has been on the development of skills and abilities in members of community groups; discussion now moves on to look more widely at how community leadership can be supported and developed. Strong communities will require effective leadership that ideally is accountable, accessible and inspiring. In particular, to achieve strong communities that are, for example, *active, organised* and *participative*, the process will need people who as leaders encourage involvement and build bridges, rather than hold power and resources for their own ends. Part Two explores the meaning of community leadership and how it can be supported to help to build stronger communities.

Any geographical area is likely to have a layer of local leadership made up of active people from a variety of sectors and settings; Box 2.10 describes a range of these.

Box 2.10 Community leaders

Community leaders may have a wide range of roles such as:

- Chairpersons of residents' associations
- Faith-based leaders
- Community activists

▶

◀

- Environmental campaigners
- Town and parish councillors
- Trustees of local charities
- Elected members of local authorities
- Representatives of service users
- Representatives of communities of interest
- Representatives of networks of community groups
- Organisers of online networks
- Editors of local newspapers and blogs
- Sports coaches

As community leaders, these individuals may be paid or unpaid, elected or selected and in different ways be representative of the area. Some may have formal leadership roles, such as chairperson, whilst many will, in effect, be leaders but without any title or identifiable role. Some leaders can be self-appointed, assuming the role just because they turn up to public meetings, such as at neighbourhood forums, often with a particular axe to grind. Also, there are those with particular status, such as local employers, who may act as leaders because of their economic power. Other types of informal leaders to consider in community settings are, for example, hairdressers, café owners and shopkeepers, who can be key channels for information flow. This is the case in Beeston, Leeds where a corner shop acts as a key hub for community involvement. Equally, in Lidgett Green in inner city Bradford, a barber shop is an important informal centre on Saturdays for older men to meet to discuss local issues.

In combination, this leadership layer, made up of formal and informal leadership roles, can be a considerable force contributing to the level of community activity and organisation in an area. Some areas will have relatively low levels of leadership experience and capacity, or where leadership is out of touch, inactive and fragmented. Others may be better organised and more accountable, ideally with leaders who are honest, confident and accessible, and, in combination, representative of both majority and minority needs.

'On our estate, we just don't have many community groups or much leadership experience.'

(Community activist, Salford)

Many people act as leaders but are under-recognised by their community. This lack of recognition can even be by the individuals themselves, who may not perceive themselves as leaders. This may be due to cultural reasons, where leadership roles may traditionally be ascribed to a limited circle, such as a group of elders or only men. It can also be due to personal reasons, such as a lack of confidence, which means that people are reluctant to see themselves in this kind of role.

In addition, the whole concept of leadership has negative perceptions in many communities. Some people feel cheated by leaders in their areas, who have benefited personally from their position. Often the experience is that leadership is 'done' to them; that it gets imposed from the inside by self-appointed 'loose cannons', or from the outside through projects being set up and run by professionals beyond local influence or control. In some cases, the leader is chosen by external agencies – they choose people they want to work through, rather than those who are recognised and chosen by the community itself.

A research project (Skinner and Farrar, 2009) found there were many assumptions made that influence how leadership was perceived in community groups, such as it was about being a born leader – the assumption here is that leaders are born with natural traits that most of us do not have. This was the major theory about leaders in the 1940s and 1950s, and many people still hold this assumption (Mullins, 1993). A second widely held assumption is that leadership is about being charismatic. There are many radical leaders who are often very inspiring; great charismatic leaders and heroes, such as Nelson Mandela and Gandhi, are classic examples of this. At local level, some charismatic leaders may be unaccountable and act as loose cannons. However, leadership does not have to be dependent on charisma; in the longer run, it might be a feature of leadership, but it is not an essential aspect of being a leader. Another image is that leaders are the people in control, telling others what to do; that is, to be a leader means to be 'bossy' and run the show. Such ideas, where the leader acts as 'top-down top-dog', run counter to values of equality and participation. The literature on leadership is full of assumptions that it is the individual who is the focus of leadership. These individuals can be inspiring, transformational and even empowering of others, but often the picture is that it is about leadership being based exclusively in one person. This individualistic approach does not match the needs of many people in the community sector and where there is a commitment to collective action. Finally, leadership in some cases is confused with good management. Many so-called leadership training courses are really about management skills. While there are some areas of overlap, leadership and management have different functions and it is useful to be clear about these (Skinner and Farrar, 2009).

In practice, there are several widespread and negative assumptions about leaders that affect popular understanding and attitudes to local leaders; that they are strong individuals driven by personal visions; bossy in style; efficient organisers; hungry for power; born to be great but distant from our own lives. These assumptions, and sometimes our own experience, turn many people in communities away from wanting to be called *leaders* and contributes to the disowning the term 'leader'. The way forward, however, is not to ignore the part leadership has to play in communities, but to look at leadership in new ways and explore how effective support can be provided. This chapter now explores three types of community leaders: those based in community groups, people who act as community representatives, and leaders who are elected members of local authorities.

In every case, based on the definition of strong communities, community leaders are needed who are aware of and committed to equal opportunities, value diversity and promote inclusion, themes explored further in Chapter 5.

Box 2.11 A definition of community leadership

Leadership is difficult to define. The subject of leadership has attracted a lot of academic study during the last few decades and not surprisingly there are many different approaches to the subject. Traditionally it can be seen as 'getting others to follow' (Mullins, 1993), or 'influencing others' (Northouse, 2007). The 'Liberating Leadership' model, devised for the Community Sector Coalition, provides a definition of community leadership that is different from most of those available:

'A process of inspiring, supporting, working with and influencing others in a group, team, organisation or community, based on an agreed set of principles, to achieve common goals and social change.'

(Skinner and Farrar, 2009)

This definition is important because it places leadership in the *community*, as well as in groups, teams and organisations, and promotes working *with* people, rather than attracting followers. It bases leadership on a set of *principles* – there is a strong values base – that many definitions of leadership do not have. Also, it presents leadership as aiming to achieve common, rather than individual goals, and *social change*, rather than just changes within an organisation.

Developing leadership in groups

Leadership development in communities can employ many different *forms of learning* and support as described above, such as training courses, mentoring, reviews, action learning and shadowing. In addition, there are different *approaches* to helping individuals develop their abilities as community leaders. Four of these approaches, the traits approach, the skills approach, the styles approach and the roles approach, are now explored in turn.

Strengthening traits

This approach focuses on the personal qualities of the individual leader, such as integrity, honesty and drive. The traits approach to leadership has a long history, based on the idea that organisations needed a top person with the right traits to lead effectively. Rather than develop leadership, the issue was about selecting the right person for a senior position (Mullins, 1993). The traits approach, however, became unpopular because different researchers came up with different lists of traits (Lloyd and Rothwell, 2007). Another difficulty is that the traits approach contributes to the idea that some people are born to be leaders, which can make leadership seem inaccessible to the everyday citizen.

The traits approach, however, does have its uses; from the different research, some of the key universal traits in leaders are intelligence, self-confidence, determination, integrity and sociability (Northouse, 2007). There are practical tools available to use with individuals in community settings, such as a traits questionnaire (Northouse, 2009). It is possible to strengthen traits over time – an individual, with support, can look at their own personal qualities and enhance them through reflection and discussion. Coaching and mentoring are useful learning methods here, where a practitioner can use a variety of tools to work with an individual to help them strengthen their leadership traits.

The skills approach

In contrast, the skills approach identifies leadership as consisting of certain skills and competencies. These can be usefully divided into three categories:

- *Administrative skills* – including managing resources, and 'technical competence'
- *Interpersonal skills* – such as being socially perceptive, showing emotional awareness and handling conflict
- *Conceptual skills* – including problem-solving, strategic planning and creating vision (Northouse, 2009).

Many of the methods for identifying learning needs described earlier could be applied when working with individuals to help them strengthen their leadership skills. One particular skill area that is very relevant for community leaders concerns the art of decision-making. Various rather complex models of decision-making have been developed (Mullins, 1993). Box 2.12 describes a range of options developed by the author especially for leaders of community groups.

Box 2.12 Decision-making in community groups

A leader of a group has a range of options to choose from in carrying out effective decision-making to help the group to achieve its aims. Many leaders prefer to choose a participative approach, which involves all group members in making the decision, either through consensus or majority vote. However, situations arise where it may be necessary or more effective for the leader to make the decision themselves. For instance, to take an extreme example, if the building catches fire, do not call a meeting, call the fire brigade! In other cases, it may be appropriate for the leader, through discussion and agreement with the group, to delegate the decision to a smaller number of people, such as a working group, which is either given the capacity to get on with the decisions or to develop a proposal to bring back to the group for their approval. The leader, in effect, has a menu of at least six possibilities:

Decision-making Menu

- Make the decision alone, then inform the group

- Consult the group, then decide on your own

- Involve the group in decision-making through majority vote

- Involve the group in decision-making through consensus

- Delegate the issue to a working group for them to prepare a proposal to bring back to the whole group for their decision

- Delegate the issue to a working group for them to make the decision on their own.

▶

◀

Practitioners can work with leaders to help them think through their choices for different decisions and whether they are making the best choices. A common complaint in community groups is that the chairperson makes too many decisions on their own between meetings. Equally, the practitioner can support the group to understand when the leader may need to make decisions quickly on their own, or just consult one or two committee members.

Choosing leadership styles

The discussion on decision-making leads on to consider the wider issue of the type of *leadership style* a leader might be adopting for different situations, either consciously or unconsciously. Leadership style is about behaviours and the way the leadership functions are carried out (Mullins, 1993). Three different styles have been called authoritarian, democratic and laissez-faire (Northouse, 2009), but two of these terms are rather value loaded. Alternative titles include the following:

➢ *Directive* – Leaders emphasize they are in charge and assert themselves through influencing group members. A directive leader would make decisions between meetings more frequently and argue they had the right and ability to do so. They may get more things done than other styles, but often this style will alienate others. Over time, group members may lose interest or rebel.

➢ *Laissez-faire* – At the other end of the spectrum, the leader delegates tasks and decisions to group members but shows little interest in any further developments. Laissez-faire leaders have a hands-off approach, leaving group members to largely do what they want to do. This style can stimulate activity and a sense of ownership in the group, but also feelings of being abandoned and lacking guidance.

➢ *Participative* – The leader acts as guide and facilitator, enabling group involvement in key decisions. When needed, decisions and tasks are delegated, but with appropriate follow-up and support. Such arrangements usually produce more sustained commitment from group members but may take more time and skills on the part of the leader.

These three different styles are often used unconsciously by leaders. An important insight is that the type of leadership style can be chosen, depending on the situation the leader is facing. A crisis, such as the community centre being broken into, might well require directive leadership without time for delegation or debate. By contrast, a strongly delegated way of working, moving towards laissez-faire, might be useful as a group learning method. While the descriptions of the three basic styles given above are generalisations, using a particular style to match a particular situation can be very effective, and has been the subject of extensive study (Schedlitzki and Edwards, 2014).

Practitioners can help leaders to consider their use of different styles in different situations and when these various styles could be positive or negative in their outcome. Different styles will require different skills; for example, the participative style of leadership will often require effective facilitation skills.

Leadership roles

A very different approach to understanding leadership is based on the concept of *leadership roles*. This approach looks more at developing effective leadership as a function within the group, rather than just focusing on the traits, skills or styles of the individual. By describing leadership as a set of roles, it is also a way of approaching what is called shared or 'distributed' leadership. Minzberg developed a 'model of managing' that includes a range of roles, or functions, carried out by leaders. His range of leadership roles is especially useful as the roles focus on the environment of the organisation, as well as on internal processes (Minzberg, 2013). Minzberg's roles are, however, still based in the setting of large corporate organisations. In contrast, research carried out for the Community Sector Coalition identified a number of roles that were observable in community groups. This work also led to a tool kit and new model called 'Liberating Leadership', which included the proposal of 10 roles to describe leadership in community groups (Skinner and Farrar, 2009). Each of the roles describes a different *function* that can be carried out by people who are members of community groups:

- Facilitator   Representative
- Questioner   Leadership Builder
- Bridge Builder   Campaigner
- Catalyst   Team Builder
- Entrepreneur   Coordinator

Box 2.13 gives a description of each leadership role. These roles operate in combination with the more formal roles of chairperson or treasurer and are not intended as a replacement. Any one group may only have a limited number of the 10 roles being carried out, such as Facilitator, Coordinator and Campaigner. Some of the leadership roles are based in the group but are mainly carried on outside the group in the community.

In many cases, the mix of active leadership roles in a community group will be appropriate for the type of group and its aims. In other cases, some valuable roles may be missing that the group would benefit from having. Often roles will be concentrated in one person who may be doing too much, leaving others out and end up exhausted. Alternatively, roles might be all concentrated in one person because other group members are over-relying on them to do everything. One way forward is for more roles to be spread out amongst several group members.

This set of roles helps us understand leadership as range of *functions* that happen in community groups. This is in contrast, for example, to the *traits* approach, which focuses on the individual and their personal qualities. The set of roles means that leadership can be more easily recognised by people in groups; it reflects what people are in reality already doing but making this more explicit. Through this recognition, leadership in groups can be supported and strengthened. Practitioners can use the set of roles to develop leadership, working with *individuals*. The set of 10 roles can be used with individual group members to look at the existing roles they carry out and any support needs related to them. Are they happy with the mix of roles they carry out? Do they feel confident in all the roles they carry out? Through this review, a leader might discover that they are carrying out a very wide range of roles too demanding for them. The set of 10 leadership roles in Box 2.13 can also be used with *groups*. The list of roles can be used by groups to look at how different roles are, in effect, allocated between members. This can help the group be clearer about who is doing what and, if appropriate, could involve increasing the spread of leadership roles in the group. Further options are given below.

The mix of roles operating in any group will vary depending on needs. The roles mix will look very different in a community centre committee than in, say, an arts group. The range of roles in a group might also change over time; sometimes there can be joint leadership and, at other times, leadership roles will be more effective if concentrated in one person. The pattern might change as new projects are taken on and the group goes through different stages in its lifetime. In some cases, leadership roles will, in effect, be shared between staff and volunteer members, for example, in a management committee with a paid worker.

Notes

The Liberating Leadership tool kit can be down loaded for free from the author's website: www.steveskinnerassociates.org.uk

The set of 10 leadership roles in community groups described in Box 2.13 is not a theory of *team roles*, for example, such as that developed by Myers-Briggs (www.myersbriggs.org) which looks at personality types, drawing from psychological research, or by Belbin (www.belbin.com) which explores the different ways team members behave, contribute and interrelate.

Box 2.13 Ten Leadership Roles in Community Groups

Role	Activities
Facilitator	Consulting and involving others in the group in decision-making, planning and problem-solving. Facilitating discussion on key issues, looking at new ways to involve people in decision-making. Ensuring everyone has a chance to contribute.
Questioner	Acting as a leader who questions and challenges attitudes and practices that discriminate against people. Working in ways to involve marginalised groups and people who feel left out or are excluded.
Bridge Builder	Reaching out, building links, contact and understanding between people from different organisations, cultures and identities. Valuing differences in traditions and faiths, breaking down isolation and challenging prejudice. Developing relationships for effective partnership working, whilst not losing sight of the values and aims of the group.
Catalyst	Promoting and involving the group in seeing the sustainable way ahead. Offering different ideas and experiences for positive change. Helping to identify the changes needed in the group to achieve the collectively agreed long-term aim.
Entrepreneur	Developing new ideas, thinking boldly and creatively, considering the pros and cons of different possibilities with the group. Taking action and starting new projects and activities, based on collectively agreed decisions.
Representative	Being informed by local needs to act as a representative, upholding values and reporting back effectively. Speaking up for and championing for the group. Acting as an 'advocate' on a particular need or issue. Using different ways to be accountable to the group.
Leadership Builder	Supporting and providing opportunities for people to get involved in activities that will build confidence and their own strengths as leaders. Supporting others to take on leadership roles in the group. Developing their own and others' knowledge, skills and abilities as leaders, starting from strengths.
Campaigner	Organising for the changes needed in the neighbourhood and wider community, based on the group's common goals. Acting on the group's views on local issues.
Team Builder	Working with the group to create a team that works well together. Helping to resolve conflict and disputes in the group.
Coordinator	Taking a lead in planning and organising events, activities and projects. Helping to ensure the resources and money needed for the agreed plan will be available.

Box 2.14 Mapping leadership roles

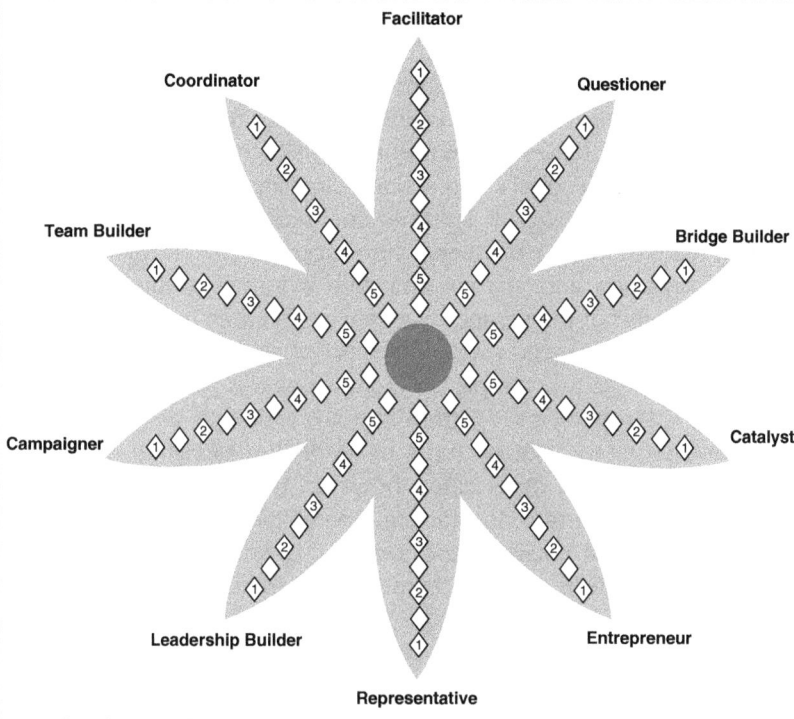

Facilitator

Coordinator

Questioner

Team Builder

Bridge Builder

Campaigner

Catalyst

Leadership Builder

Entrepreneur

Representative

Level one	This role is not carried out in or by our group
Level two	This role is carried out to a minor extent
Level three	This role is carried out to some extent
Level four	This role is carried out to a large extent
Level five	This role is carried out fully

Strengthening leadership within the group

The framework of 10 leadership roles is included here so that both practitioners and leaders can better understand how leadership is functioning in community groups and how leadership can be strengthened. By focusing on leadership as a set of roles, it makes the work of building more effective leadership more accessible.

Practitioners can help groups to look at how different leadership roles are being carried out among group members. The mapping chart in Box 2.14 can be used with groups to help them identify the current spread of leadership roles. Each arm in the chart represents one of the leadership roles. The chart can be copied, and each group member be invited to complete it, showing for each arm the level at which they think that role is being carried out in the group. The different interpretations in each person's chart can then be discussed through feedback and action points agreed on.

To carry out this activity, it is important that the group is interested in developing leadership and has been introduced to the set of roles already. Also, the chairperson and anyone else with a formal group role needs to understand the aims of the session in advance and agree to participate.

Some groups may function well with most or all of the 10 leadership roles carried out by one or two people. In many cases this system works well; for example, this is the traditional pattern in many residents' associations, where the chair and secretary take on most or all of the leadership roles through their formal positions. In other cases, however, the group may benefit from adopting a different pattern. In practice, one or two people may be holding too many roles, which could be too demanding for them and exclude others from using their skills and talents more. Spreading roles in the group can encourage more members to take the initiative or at least support someone else carrying out a role, depending on their interests, skills and experience. In the current climate, many groups are keen to strengthen the bridge-building role and ensure it is given proper support and encouragement.

In carrying this out exercise, it is important not to assume an increased sharing of roles is necessarily the best arrangement. The advantages and disadvantages of increasing the spread of roles can be debated. In practice, the group may decide to keep the spread of roles as they are.

Where changes are needed, a new large map can be created on a flip chart with names against various roles, based on collectively agreed decisions about who is doing what in future. This can lead to greater clarity about the delegation of roles. Even without changing the existing spread of roles, a group might wish to have two people carrying out any one role. This can generate greater involvement and skill development; the key thing is to ensure there is clarity of who is doing what and why.

As mentioned, this set of leadership roles is not intended to substitute for formal roles that may exist in a community group, such as chairperson, but can help to add greater clarity to the informal leadership functions being carried out. Whatever changes the group may want, the key objective is to achieve greater clarity as to who is carrying out which roles and that each individual has appropriate support to do this. Creating a situation where roles are blurred and unclear is definitely to be avoided.

Community representatives

Community representatives are people who are involved in decision-making in partnerships and consultative bodies to influence policy and practice in public services and neighbourhoods. They will be involved because they are selected or elected by a network of groups, service users or residents, selected by a partnership or consultative body, or self-selected, having appointed themselves to act on behalf of a wider group, network or community. Community representatives selected by their particular network are likely to be more accountable but can be under pressure to 'represent' a wider body of people. For example, one person from a network of visually impaired groups can be expected to act on behalf of a range of disability groups across the city.

Community representatives have a number of tasks to carry out, such as the collection of views and information on their network's or group's concerns and the dissemination of information on key decisions to group or network members. Often representatives feel under pressure to respond quickly to opportunities to have a say about new proposals but need time to go back to their networks to gather views. A further challenge is where representatives get involved in the policy agendas of the partnership and engage with the needs of its members, which over time may lead to a distance growing between them and their own base-camp networks. Getting the balance right on these issues is a challenging dilemma.

Research carried out for the National Association for Voluntary and Community Action (NAVCA) identified four key activities for community representatives, based on representatives involved in district-wide, strategic partnerships (Skinner and Mitchell, 2008). The four key activities were the following: 1) *Being a voice* – taking issues of concern to the partnership, acting as a bridge and ensuring many voices are heard; feeding back to third-sector groups and communities and involving them in consultation. 2) *Influencing decisions* – challenging and supporting proposals; acting as a critical friend; influencing the thinking of people who make decisions. 3) *Building the partnership*, through improving arrangements and the overall quality of work, thus helping to direct resources to greatest effect, was also a key activity. 4) *Promoting the sector* was an important activity, ensuring partners are aware of the particular contribution of the third sector; bringing knowledge of community groups and what they have to offer.

Other key responsibilities identified in this research included feeding back information to other voluntary sector groups, standing up for the sector whilst maintaining good relationships, analysing complex documents and influencing decisions – in total quite a demanding list! Similarly, research into the skills needed by community representatives identified an extensive list, falling under three main headings of people skills, practical skills and partnership skills, as described in Resource Two. Practitioners can support community representatives by helping them to identify their learning needs, using methods described earlier. The list of skills in Resource Two can be used as a menu to support individuals who wish to strengthen their abilities. Practitioners can also promote training courses for community representatives. These can cover a range of skills and abilities, for example, using the framework in Resource Two.

In 2012, the Wakefield Assembly, a network of voluntary and community sector organisations, organised a six-month training programme called 'Creating Stronger Voices', which was designed and delivered by the author. Participants came from a wide range of networks and groups, and the aim was to 'create a stronger strategic voice in local decision-making'. The sessions included the art of being a community representative; leadership skills; partnership and team working skills; confidence building; assertiveness training; and how to influence public sector organisations. The course was participative in style, combining presentations, exercises, feedback, group discussions, handouts and sign-posting to further materials. The final session included a visiting speaker from a neighbouring local authority.

Elected members as community leaders

The current economic climate throws up many challenges for front-line elected members in local government, requiring relationships with communities that may be different from the more traditional ones. New, more creative approaches to local government are needed. In 'Rebalancing the Power', a research report by New Local Government Network, and supported by Local Trust, five guiding principles for successful relationships between councils and communities are described. These are based on research carried out in Big Local areas funded by the Big Lottery. These neighbourhoods are a unique microcosm in which the new dynamic between councils and communities was identified (Tjoa, 2018).

Across the country, in this changing environment, many elected members of all parties are interested in acting more as 'community leaders' in their local areas. A new set of six roles for elected members devised by the author describes what this could mean in practice. This set of roles was developed through dis-cussion with a wide range of councillors and officers over several years as part of the Local Government Information Unit's seminar series on community engage-ment. The set of six roles also draw on a useful set of political skills developed by the Local Government Association (Silvester, 2013). The six roles for elected members are enabling decision-making, enabling action, building bridges, man-aging local resources, joint working and enhancing community capacity. While the six leadership roles for elected members are briefly introduced here, more information on the roles is in Resource Three, later in this book.

Crucial to their unique contribution is that elected members bring demo-cratic legitimacy to the table, potentially balancing up the needs of all parts of their community. It is important also that officers in local authorities under-stand the type of leadership roles that elected members may wish to use in their front-line work and can support them in these roles. The set of six roles can help elected members to build stronger communities in their areas. It is not in any way suggested that any one elected member needs to carry out all six roles; the set of six roles is presented as a 'menu' to choose from, depend-ing on preferences and local needs.

As a framework, the six roles can be used by elected members, with support from officers, to look at how to plan their work over the coming year. They are a resource to draw on and to be used in a flexible way. They are not in any way intended as a substitute for the existing roles that members have as political representatives of their wards, which involve core political skills, although there is some inevitable overlap. The six roles for elected members as community leaders draw on but are different from the 10 leadership roles described earlier, which are specifically based in the setting of community groups. In contrast the six roles are a distinct set developed to describe the particular setting of being an elected member. See Resource Three for more material.

Summary

Chapter 2 has introduced some key material on supporting individuals through learning and development; it looked at:

➢ Ways to identify learning needs in community groups

➢ Different forms of community-based learning

➤ The nature of community leadership

➤ Leadership roles in community groups, with 10 of these identified

➤ Skills for community representatives

➤ Elected members as community leaders, with six main roles.

The main points have been:

➤ Start by recognising and valuing existing abilities and strengths.

➤ In the current climate, the learning needs of community groups are changing, as, for example, many are involved in campaigns to save their local services.

➤ Different forms of learning have different advantages and disadvantages.

➤ *Building people* is not just about structured, more formal community-based learning but also about using informal, creative approaches.

➤ Developing effective leadership is a key part of strengthening communities.

➤ A set of 10 leadership roles is a useful way to describe leadership functions in community groups; they could be adapted and reduced in number to address different settings and needs.

➤ Elected members have valuable parts to play in strengthening communities, and a set of six leadership roles helps to describe this.

➤ *Building people* is a shared approach that involves valuing what each person has to offer and jointly building confidence and abilities.

➤ Everyone will have their own journey to make, and talents to bring.

In terms of the definition of stronger communities introduced in Chapter 1, *building people* will contribute to developing communities that, in particular, are *active, participative* and *organised*.

Developing your practice

Useful questions to consider are:

➤ In your own life, what particular forms of learning have had most impact on you? For example, courses, mentoring, visits, reading?

➤ What barriers do you have about participating in learning?

➢ Looking back, what have been some of the key elements of your own learning journey?

➢ In supporting other people's learning, how can you help people to identify their learning needs?

➢ How have learning needs changed in grass roots communities over the last few years, given the levels of destitution and poverty that exist in modern Britain?

➢ What are your experiences of leaders in your own community?

➢ What are the three most important traits of an effective community leader?

➢ How could you help community groups to develop their leadership abilities?

➢ Can you think of an example when you, in effect, acted in a leadership role? Was this appropriate?

➢ What does the set of 10 group leadership roles mean to you?

➢ How can you strengthen leadership in communities in ways that are empowering?

➢ How can you strengthen leadership in communities based on the values of equal opportunities, diversity and inclusion?

For practitioners, it is important not to assume that group members and community leaders need to develop their abilities but the practitioner does not! Whatever your role, this publication aims to support you in your own journey of developing further skills and abilities, appreciating what you already know and can do. *Building people* needs to be a shared approach, valuing what each person has to offer, and jointly building confidence and abilities.

Resources

The Liberating Leadership tool kit can be downloaded for free from the
    author's website www.steveskinnerassociates.org.uk
www.cldstandardscouncil.org.uk
www.creativepeopleplaces.org.uk/our-learning/shared-decision-making-toolkit
www.creativepeopleplaces.org.uk/our-learning/mapping-and-analysis-of-
    engagement-approaches
www.chex.org.uk/health-issues-community-hiic/hiic-tutor-resources/
www.communitygames.org.uk/toolkit

www.networkedcity.london/livinglab
www.futurelearn.com/
www.mensshedscymru.co.uk/
www.superslowway.org.uk/projects/shapes-of-water-sounds-of-hope/
www.infed.org/
www.nationalcan.ning.com
www.wevolution.org.uk
www.localtrust.org.uk
www.freire.org

References: Chapter 2

Ali, Y. (2018) *Using a Freirean Approach within the Global Youth Solutions Programme* in Melling, A. and Pilkington, R. (eds) *Paulo Freire and Transformative Education: Changing Lives and Transforming Communities*. London: Palgrave Macmillan.

Anderton, A. (2018) *Together We Are Bradford*. Bradford: CNet.

Burns, P. (2011) *Entrepreneurship and Small Business Start-Up, Growth and Maturity*. London: Red Globe Press.

Farrar, G., Smith, T. and Farrar, M. (2017) *Celebrate! 50 Years of Leeds West Indian Carnival*. Huddersfield: Northern Arts Publications.

Freire, P. (1972) *Pedagogy of the Oppressed*. New York: Herder and Herder.

Honey, P. and Mumford, A. (1982) *The Learning Styles Manual*. Maidenhead: Peter Honey Publications.

Ireland, T. (2018) *The Relevance of Freire for the Post-2015 International Debate on Development and Education and the Role of Popular Education* in Melling, A. and Pilkington, R. (eds) *Paulo Freire and Transformative Education: Changing Lives and Transforming Communities*. London: Palgrave Macmillan.

Kirkwood, G. and Kirkwood, C. (2011) *Living Adult Education: Freire in Scotland*. Rotterdam: Sense Publishers.

Kolb, D. (1984) *Experiential Learning*. Englewood Cliffs, NJ: Prentice Hall.

Ledwith, M. (2011) *Community Development: A Critical Approach*. 2nd ed. Bristol: Policy Press.

Ledwith, M. (2016) *Community Development in Action: Putting Freire into Practice*. Bristol: Policy Press.

Lloyd, M. and Rothwell, B. (2007) *Leadership 101*. London: Directory of Social Change.

Minzbeg, H. (2013) *Simply Managing*. San Fransisco: Berrett-Koehler Publishers Inc.

Mullins, L. (1993) *Management and Organisational Behaviour*. London: Pitman Publishing.

Northouse, P. (2007) *Leadership Theory and Practice*. 2007. California: Sage Publications.

Northouse, P. (2009) *Introduction to Leadership Concepts and Practice*. California: Sage Publications.

O'Hara, A., Weber, Z. and Levine, K. (2016) *Skills for Human Service Practice: Working with Individuals, Groups and Communities*. Oxford: Oxford University Press.

Schedlitzki, D. and Edwards, G. (2014) *Studying Leadership*. London: Sage.

Schutz, A and Sandy, M. (2011) *Collective Action for Social Change*. New York: Palgrave Macmillan.

Silvester, J. (2013) *The Political Skills Framework: A Councillor's Toolkit*. London: Local Government Association.

Skinner, S. and Farrar, G. (2009) *Liberating Leadership*. London: Community Sector Coalition.

Skinner, S. and Mitchell, L. (2008) *Skilling up for Stronger Voices*. Sheffield: NAVCA.

Thompson, N. (2006) *Promoting Workplace Learning*. Bristol: Policy Press.

Tjoa, P. (2018) *Rebalancing the Power: Five Principles for a Successful Relationship between Councils and Communities*. London: New Local Government Network.

Twelvetrees, A. (2017) *Community Development, Social Action and Social Planning*. London: Red Globe Press.

Whiddett, S. and Hollyforde, S. (2003) *A Practical Guide to Competencies*. London: Chartered Institute of Personal and Development.

3

Building Organisations

Chapter 2 looked at supporting individuals; in contrast, this chapter focuses on supporting community groups and voluntary organisations. Across the country, small-scale community groups and voluntary organisations provide the bedrock of community life. Many receive grants from public sources and also raise their own funds or generate their income; some are unfunded and informally organised. In combination, they provide a tremendous range of activities and services, often with little publicity or wider recognition. *Building organisations*, one of the four central themes in this book, is a key part of the work of strengthening communities, so that voluntary organisations and community groups at the grass roots can be more *active* and *organised*. This chapter is about how practitioners can support and strengthen voluntary organisations and community groups, so they can be even more effective in achieving their aims, based on the key assumption that they want such help, rather than having it imposed upon them.

The potential range of ways to support community groups and voluntary organisations is very broad, such as helping them to:

➢ Run effective events and meetings

➢ Work well as a team and resolve conflicts

➢ Address equal opportunities and diversity issues

➢ Involve different parts of the community

➢ Recruit and manage volunteers and staff

➢ Manage money, buildings and resources

➢ Adopt appropriate structures

➢ Run projects

➢ Work well with other organisations

➢ Communicate effectively

➢ Influence decisions on local issues

➢ Challenge discrimination and the misuse of power

➢ Run campaigns well.

Within this broad range of needs, this chapter focuses on helping community groups and voluntary organisations to become clearer about where they are going and look at how they are organised. The material can also be used to help groups to create a plan to change and develop over the coming months or years and more effectively organise new projects and activities. In many cases, such support will not involve groups changing their organisational structure, such as becoming a charity or limited company, but developing in more practical ways, as discussed below. After an introduction on the nature of community groups, Part One of this chapter looks at working with and supporting individual groups. Part Two then focuses on supporting a number of groups where they are joining together across a geographical area or network. Both forms of support – individual and collective – are explored in this chapter.

A practitioner's work needs to be guided by a clear set of values and may well involve challenging groups, especially where they are engaging in prejudice and discrimination. Supporting groups and organisations through growth and change can be demanding, requireing certain specialised skills (Mullins, 1993). How practitioners can build their own skills and ways of working is discussed below. Please note that rather than keep repeating the term *community groups and voluntary organisations*, the term 'community group' is used from here onwards, reflecting also that this book's main focus is on small-scale, community sector organisations and groups.

Community groups

Community groups carry out a wide range of valuable functions in communities. Groups can be made up, for example, of residents, service users and local volunteers. In some cases, they will involve staff who work for the group. They are often an accessible way for people to get involved in activities and act as volunteers, as they provide a great many activities and informal services and are often a central part of community life. As well as groups that are made up mainly of residents, many people join together as a community of interest or identity, as explored in Chapter 1. In 2016, there were over 100,000 registered small charities in England and Wales, nearly 80% of all charities. Around half of all small charities have an income between £1 and £10,000 (NCVO, 2016). The focus of this book, however, is more on small-scale community sector groups, many of which are not charities or incorporated. This grass-roots layer of community groups and activities can be categorised as 'below the radar', and it is under-researched (Phillimore et al., 2010). There are large variations between different areas, with some areas having well-organised community groups that seem to be successful in running activities and improving things. Other areas appear to lack many groups, and those that exist are poorly organised and struggling to achieve their aims.

Key roles for groups are not only running a range of local events and activities but also having a say about local issues and influencing decisions about their own community. Also, some groups may be independently delivering services commissioned by public bodies, while others are working in partnerships. In many rural areas, parish councils and village halls are often the hub of local community activity. Many community groups are based in buildings, such as a community centre, while others are network based, such as a federation of disability groups. Increasingly, social-media-based local groups are an important part of community life. Some areas also have locally based federations or similar bodies that bring together a range of local groups such as tenants' associations. Most local authority districts or boroughs have a list of groups and voluntary organisations, produced by a district-wide, voluntary sector organisation, such as a Council for Voluntary Services, often known as 'Voluntary Action'.

Part One: supporting individual groups

There are many ways to support groups and help them form and develop, described very effectively by existing writers (Twelvetrees, 2017). Supporting community groups in the context of strengthening communities is about helping them to achieve their aims. This approach to supporting and empowering grass-roots groups focuses on what groups themselves want to do, rather than the agenda originating from public service providers.

Community groups may feel they need help for a variety of reasons, such as applying to a new funding programme or starting a different activity. Help could also be needed due to negative factors, such as internal conflicts, members leaving, or the chairperson resigning suddenly, or due to positive reasons, such as an opportunity to take on running a building. Such reasons can be internally or externally driven. In some cases, the problem grows slowly over time, where a group might not be aware that they need to develop and change; however, the practitioner can help them to realise this.

Groups have choices on how they can seek help; they could ask one of their own members or members of another group for help, which has the advantage of making use of grass-roots experience and skills. Alternatively, they could invite a practitioner they know already, such as a local community worker, or invite a practitioner they do not know. If they are part of a membership organisation, such as a council for voluntary service or national voluntary sector organisation, specialist help may be available. If they have a budget, they could recruit a paid specialist. There's always another option – ignore the issue and muddle through!

Each option will have different advantages and disadvantages for the group. The last option – muddling through – is to be avoided! The first option, of asking one of their own members to help, is generally not recommended because, more than likely, the existing group member will be too close to the issues to see the problem clearly and even be part of the problem (Paton and McCalman, 2000).

'Some groups don't realise they need help until they get it!'

(Community worker, South Wales)

Initial support for a group from a practitioner they know already could be just to help them choose the right person to assist them and write a clear brief, as described below. In working with community groups, bear in mind that many will already be effective at what they want to do but may have just strayed from their original aims and only need a limited amount of help to get back on track. They may already have the capacity to do what they now want to do but need some help to realise this. It is also misleading to assume groups always need to proceed from being small scale and informally structured to being large, more complex, incorporated organisations. Equally, in the current climate, many groups are reviewing their traditional roles and want to take on new challenges.

Helping groups to identify their needs and strengths

Some community groups may only need 'light-touch' help, for example the practitioner providing information on funding sources or giving advice and guidance, such as how the council works. The support could involve the facilitation of an occasional meeting or event to deal with issues before they grow too unmanageable, giving contacts to people in the voluntary sector and in the public services, or linking groups with other community organisations.

Such light-touch help may be all that is needed; indeed, avoiding the situation where the group becomes overdependent on the practitioner is important. Linking groups with each other, where they share information and skills, can also be a useful way forward, rather than assuming the solution lies outside the community sector. In other cases, groups will request and need more substantial forms of support, and it is crucial at an early stage to establish clearly what the problem, need or opportunity is that they want to address. The group may be clear from the start about what they need, or instead, not be at all clear on what the problems are and require some initial discussion to clarify this. They may have an idea what the cause of the problem is but further probing from the practitioner unearths other issues.

The first issue is to help the group to identify what is needed, rather than immediately come up with a 'solution', or just assume the answer is an 'away-day' or applying for a grant. Bear in mind, the issue or need the group initially presents to you as the 'problem' could be only the tip of the iceberg; equally, the person who contacts you to request your help may not represent the rest of the group's view of what is needed or even be the main problem!

One way to help clarify needs is by using a menu. For example, Box 3.1 has a menu of organisational elements that community groups may find useful. This list will need to be adapted and used in a selective way, depending on the type of group; that is why it is presented here as a *menu*, rather than a *checklist*. It is a pick and mix resource and is *not* in any way intended as a blueprint for all community groups.

Box 3.1 A menu for a healthy community organisation

Values – an appropriate set of underlying beliefs

Aims – a clear set of aims and objectives and vision of the future

Strategy – a long-term action plan on how to achieve the aims

Organisation – a constitution or terms of reference

Structure – a decision-making body, such as a committee, and/or legal structure, such as a trust or limited company

Policies – for example, on equal opportunities, using volunteers, managing staff, and financial reporting

Practices – arrangements for the use of space, handling petty cash and equipment, and recruiting and involving people

Leadership – individuals who coordinate action, understand their role, ensure delivery, exercise effective control when needed, are outward and forward looking and empower other people

Skills and abilities – trustees, members, staff and volunteers equipped with appropriate knowledge, skills and ways of working

Resources – volunteers, contacts, equipment, buildings, space, contracts, stocks and cash reserves

▶

◀

Finances – systems of recording and managing income and expenditure in an accountable manner; managing cash flow effectively

Communications – ways of contacting, consulting and informing users, members, volunteers, residents and networks, including the effective use of social media

Relationships – good working relationships with members, staff, neighbours, other groups, stakeholders, funders and authorities

A key point to bear in mind is the need to be *flexible*; any one group may not need help with all or even most of the elements in Box 3.1. As mentioned earlier, it is important that practitioners do not impose changes and new systems that are inappropriate.

In meeting and observing the group, you will need to consider diversity issues. Is the group based in a particular faith or culture? What traditions and beliefs need to be considered in understanding how the group operates? You will also need to consider equal opportunities. Are some group members dominating the conversation? Are some people being left out? Are some people alienated from the group? Part of the art of being an effective practitioner is to expect anything and be prepared to respond on the hoof!

Developing a brief

As a practitioner, you may be asked to support a group to address the issues, needs or concerns identified through initial discussion. At an early point in the process, it is worth putting the main points down in writing; this can be called an agreement or 'brief'.

Box 3.2 Useful questions to cover in a brief

- What issue or need is the group addressing?
- What is the aim of the support?
- What type of help can the practitioner provide?
- Who will be involved?
- How much time is involved?
- What costs are involved, if any?
- What is the planned outcome?

▶

◀

- Who will type up notes from any sessions held?
- Is the aim to produce a long-term strategy for the group?
- Is the aim to design a new project?
- Is the aim to produce an action plan?
- How will the group keep control of the process?
- How will the practitioner report back to the group?
- Will the practitioner share any of their skills with the group?
- How will the group evaluate the impact of the support?

Not all these questions may need to be addressed; the level of detail will vary. The key thing is to establish a clear agreement with the group at an early stage about the type and amount of help the practitioner can provide.

Choosing your approach

There are many different approaches to working with groups through processes of planning and development. Here are two contrasting ones, both of which have clear benefits:

➤ *Research-based support* – Here a practitioner, once the brief is agreed, carries out a fact-finding process by doing desk-based research. This could involve looking at minutes of meetings, existing procedures and policies, reports and the constitution. The research could include interviewing all group members, each staff member and/or key stakeholders and then combining the data collected to produce a set of findings. If relevant, the research could include looking at different organisational structures for a group, such as becoming a limited company or community interest company. Having carried out the research, the practitioner then presents a report to the group, with a set of proposals for changes and improvements.

➤ *Facilitation-based support* – Here a practitioner organises a session or series of group sessions and uses facilitation methods to bring out the groups' views, knowledge and insights on the need, problem or opportunity being addressed. Proposals are developed in a collective way, with the practitioner having little or no more influence than anyone else. Notes and action points can be written up as the basis of future change.

The research-based approach has the advantage of bringing new hard and soft data to the group, and it is a relatively objective view on the way forward. However, a major drawback of the research-based approach is that the group may feel a lack of ownership of the proposals for change. The research-based support may present an informed solution to the problem or need but generate little enthusiasm.

Facilitation-based approaches, by contrast, are more likely to generate a sense of ownership and involve the whole group. Equally, a criticism of the facilitation-based approach is that it merely uses existing information and views that the group already has, rather than bringing in anything new or additional. Given the brief or problem facing the group, it may be obvious which one to use. Often a combination of both approaches is the best solution, where an initial period of research can be followed up with facilitated sessions. This chapter mostly focuses on the facilitation-based approach, because based on the author's experience, it is more likely to bring about lasting change in groups and will be a more empowering experience for group members. Research on change management has also indicated the importance of the psychological aspect of change, where new behaviours are required, but often resisted by participants (Blake and Bush, 2009).

Whatever approach is used, it will be important for the practitioner to build up trust and get to know the group and its key members. Being introduced at an early stage to everyone involved will be useful if the practitioner is not known to them already. The practitioner will also need to discuss with the group exactly who will be involved as participants in the review process, and this will vary depending on the nature of the group and the extent of its membership. Options to consider are:

➤ The immediate decision-making body, committee or board

➤ The wider membership of the group, if any

➤ Volunteers who help out (if different from the membership)

➤ Users of the group's services

➤ Participants in the group's activities and events

➤ Residents who live in the group's local area

➤ Any staff employed by the group

➤ Key stakeholders, such as the local council, funders and neighbouring groups.

For facilitation-based approaches, the participants will probably need some sheltered time away from the daily pressures in order to focus fully. A different building or room, or at least different room layout from how meetings usually happen, is important. In choosing a venue, there are practical issues to consider: Is there space for a circle of chairs or café style seating, as well as, if needed, areas for small groups to work in? Can flip charts be displayed on walls? Do you need any equipment other than a flip chart? Will there be refreshments? Is the building accessible? Will all group members be able to get there? It is vital to visit the venue in advance of the first session to check on the space and facilities available, as well as arriving early on the day.

Facilitating change in groups

For the actual facilitation work to bring about change and development in community groups, a set of *key questions* that addresses the agreed brief can be very effective. A range of such key questions is presented below, as a resource to draw on in a flexible, tailor-made way, depending on what the group needs.

> In each case, the key question is followed by a further set of secondary questions to select from for use in sessions with a group.

> These key questions are designed to be used and adapted for use with groups, without any implication that every group should need to work on all the key questions.

> For some groups, just using one key question and its secondary questions, will be enough to move them on.

> Some groups may need to respond to only two or three key questions.

> They are labelled A–O for clarity. It must be emphasised that they may, in practice, be used in a different order, depending on the needs of the group you are working with.

The key questions can be used either to help develop longer-term plans with the group or, alternatively, to enhance the design and delivery of shorter-term projects. Choose from the list and use them in a flexible way, based on what the group needs. They can be used in combination with particular organisational change *methods*, and some references to such methods are given below. Some of the key questions presented here are partly based on an excellent planning cycle with six stages, described in *Tools for Tomorrow* (2012), but mostly they come from the author's own experience.

The key questions

> *Key Question A: AIMS – What are we trying to achieve?*

Many groups set themselves up with a clear direction but then drift away over time. The original leaders may have moved on and new members are now unclear about the longer-term aims. New opportunities can cause a shift in ideas that need proper discussion; equally the original set of aims might now be seen as too narrow or too ambitious. Some issues that a practitioner could use to help the group to consider their longer-term aims are:

➤ What have we achieved so far?

➤ Why did our group start?

➤ What's our rationale for doing what we do?

➤ What were our past aims? How appropriate are these now?

➤ What is our vision now for our community or area?

➤ What do we really believe in?

➤ Which key organisations do we need to consult about our proposed aims, if any?

➤ How does the proposed new set of aims reflect our values?

Having a clear set of aims that actually means something to the group can be a real asset. It is worth keeping each aim to a maximum of one sentence in length, expressed in everyday language. Also, the term 'to' is useful here, as given in Box 3.3.

Starting by recognising and taking stock of achievements so far is a useful way to build peoples' confidence. Often a group will have a set of aims and some description of their long-term vision already written down from a few years ago, and this may just need 'refreshing' – a lovely term that usually means updating and tightening up in the current, now quite different, environment.

A different approach is to focus on *outcomes* rather than *aims*. The use of outcomes and indicators is described in LEAP, an excellent planning and evaluation framework introduced in Box 3.8 below.

Box 3.3 An example of long-term aims

This example of long-term aims comes from an organisation called CNet, based in Bradford, West Yorkshire. CNet started in 2001 as Bradford's Community Empowerment Network to support voluntary and community sector representation on the local strategic partnership – Bradford Vision. In 2007, CNet became independent as a company limited by guarantee and, in 2010, achieved charitable status. CNet is now one of the few remaining community empowerment networks in England, continuing to give a voice to local people and groups in order to influence local decision-making. This example shows CNet's set of five aims that form the basis of their work over three years from 2018:

Aim 1: To support, enable and strengthen the voice and representation of local people and groups in decision making about community issues and services. ▶

◀

Aim 2: To promote Asset-Based Community Development (ABCD) and empowerment work.

Aim 3: To develop and extend the range of services which CNet offers, based on our values.

Aim 4: To strengthen our marketing and communication on our range of services and activities.

Aim 5: To ensure the financial security and continuity of CNet.

➤ *Key Question B: VALUES – What values will guide our future?*

Values are the beliefs that underlie the group's activities, such as:

Making marginalised voices stronger

Celebrating diversity

Promoting equal opportunities

Empowering people

The role values play can be observed in various ways in groups' activities, such as to inspire people to get involved, to affect how people work together, to inform how actions are carried out and to guide the end point the group is working towards. Identifying a set of values is especially important in the current climate where groups are facing demanding challenges. Some groups just have long lists of grand sounding terms on their website, if they have one, such as 'equality', but in practice this does not mean much to individual members or website users! In facilitating groups to help them to identify a set of values, it is clearer to use verbs rather than single nouns. For example, 'Promoting equal opportunities' means more than just the word 'Equality'. Ideally the process of agreeing on a set of values will involve everyone in the group or organisation, including members, volunteers, supporters and users. Useful questions to choose from are the following:

➤ What values inspired the group to originally form?

➤ Do we have a statement of values already? Can we build on these?

➤ What motivates us to be involved?

➤ What do we really believe in about the work of this group?

➤ How will our values influence our aims and activities?

➤ What would using an equal opportunities approach mean for our activities and services?

➢ *Key Question C: NEEDS – What local needs or opportunities are we addressing?*

People often have passionate feelings about their community and want to improve conditions for the area or members. While this is admirable, they may be making assumptions about local needs with little real evidence. It is useful to take a step back with the group and to consider such questions as the following:

➢ What do we know about the needs we are concerned about?

➢ How do these needs or opportunities relate to our aims?

➢ What information do we have on the initiative we are interested in?

➢ What hopes and aspirations are we responding to?

➢ What new information do we need?

➢ Have we consulted potential beneficiaries?

➢ How will this initiative help to empower people?

➢ How will it give people a voice?

➢ How does this initiative reflect our group values?

An up-to-date review of the information the group has on the specific need or opportunity is useful. This information can be hard data, for example facts and figures on the area, or soft data, such as views held by potential beneficiaries, including their hopes and dreams for their community. It is useful to combine both hard and soft data, and in some cases, there might be a contradiction in findings between the two. For instance, household surveys may identify crime as more important than anything else, when police statistics show low crime rates.

➢ *Key Question D: ENVIRONMENT – How will the environment affect us?*

As well as the specific set of needs they want to address, the group could also consider the environment they are in, which, as discussed in Chapter 1, could now be quite different from when they started. It is crucial for groups to be aware of any cuts in public services that are happening around them and to consider options for their response:

➢ Take a stand and join a local campaign?

➢ Provide services to 'plug the gaps'?

➢ Focus on our own activities and ignore the wider picture?

A useful concept here is the term 'driver', meaning forces that shape and influence the group or organisation (Copeman and Griffith Gray, 2009). Some drivers may be predictable, while the impact of others might be uncertain. Some may be positive or negative in their impact or both. For example, hundreds of new people arriving in a village due to a new housing development may bring extra demands on local community services, as well as new skills and energies. In terms of the impact of such environmental changes, the group could consider the following:

➤ Which key drivers do we need to investigate?

➤ Which new information do we need to understand different drivers?

➤ How will we collect this information?

➤ Can we collect it ourselves or do we need outside help?

➤ What are the implications of this information on our group?

➤ What do we need to do to react to this?

Obviously, such questions cannot easily be addressed in just one session and might need research between sessions. Once the information is gathered, a picture of the key influences, barriers and the potential benefits created by the external environment can be drawn up. The impact that drivers may have on the group's future, as referred to in the last question, is especially important because research has shown that organisations can become aware of changes around them but still not react to the situation (Hayes, 2010). A useful method for identifying environmental impact is called PEST, as described in *Tools for Tomorrow* (Bruce et al., 2012).

Box 3.4 An example of drivers

CNet was introduced in Box 3.3. Their three-year strategy also included exploration of a range of different drivers in the external environment that may affect their future work, including social, technological, economic and environmental factors. From this range, particular drivers identified were the following:

• *Funding* – the move from grants to commissioning creates challenges for us.

• *Population* – the percentage of the population made up of young people is increasing.

• *Raised levels of child poverty* – many children are increasingly dependent on free school meals.

➢ *Key Question E: RESOURCES – What are our current strengths?*

The group could take stock of the general position it is in now, with an overview of its own resources. The term *resources* can include people, such as volunteers, members, advisers and leaders, as well as equipment, property, leases, contracts and finances. In taking stock, useful questions to ask the group include these:

➢ What are our current strengths in relation to our aims?

➢ What are our current weaknesses?

➢ What resources do we have to help us achieve our aims?

➢ What are our main resource gaps?

One widely used method for such stock-taking is SWOT, which stands for strengths, weaknesses, opportunities and threats, as described in Burns (2011).

➢ *Key Question F: OBJECTIVES – What are our short-term goals?*

Having considered the immediate environment and available resources, *objectives* can be seen as the stepping stones by which the group will achieve their *aims*. This is usually a longer list than the list of aims and is expressed with the term *by*, in contrast to aims, which are best described using the verb *to*. Here's an example from a community group interested in supporting young people:

Our aims as a group are:

• To improve the quality of life for young people in our neighbourhood

• To empower young people, so that they have greater control over their lives.

Our objectives are:

• By running a youth centre for young people

• By encouraging young people to manage the centre

• By giving free advice on further and higher education

• By recruiting staff who take an empowering approach.

Usually each aim will have its own matching set of objectives. In devising a set of objectives, useful questions to ask the group are:

• Is this objective achievable?

• By when will we achieve it?

- How will we measure progress and success?

- Is it specific enough in how it is described?

- Do we all agree with the proposed set of objectives?

- Do they match our set of aims?

Objectives can be presented in ways that make monitoring easier. One way to do this is by using a framework called SMARTER objectives: Objectives should be specific, measurable, achievable, reasonable, timetabled, evaluated and reviewed (Gilchrist, 2007). However, developing objectives in this way is a demanding process, takes time and may not match what members of the group want.

Box 3.5 An example of objectives

CNet also developed a set of matching objectives for each of its set of five aims. Here's one example:

Aim 1: To support, enable and strengthen the voice and representation of local people and groups in decision making about community issues and services.

Objectives

- Increase the voice of seldom heard groups, such as young people, older people, vulnerable people, people with disabilities, Eastern Europeans, and low-income families.

- Increase numbers of people in Big Local task groups.

- Further develop a range of platforms for people to make decisions about services and neighbourhoods.

➤ *Key Question G: OPTIONS – What are the best options for us to choose?*

The term 'options' used here means ways forward that a group could choose in order to achieve its objectives and longer-term aims. For example, a group that is interested in expanding its income could choose from a variety of options, such as charging for its activities when they have usually been free, raising prices for its services, diversifying its range of services, or expanding into a larger geographical area.

Options will include more detail than objectives and focus more on the 'how'. In the current climate, many community groups have become more enterprising, adopting new options to increase income from services and activities. Some members may find these changes disturbing as they can be perceived as being too business oriented. The key issue is that any options chosen still reflect the group's values and aims.

To help the group choose the most effective options, you can ask questions such as:

➢ What key options do we need to consider?

➢ What are the pros and cons of each option?

➢ What further information do we need in order to address these questions?

➢ How will our choice of option help to achieve our objectives and reflect our values?

The first question on choice of key options would require an ideas session where a wide range of possibilities is thrown up. The pros and cons of each option from the ideas session can then be explored. This second stage is a more considered process and might need some research and preparation between sessions. The comparison of pros and cons will need to consider the changing environment and the underlying set of aims.

Useful methods for identifying and comparing options are called Risk Analysis, Force Field Analysis and Twelve Strategic Options, as described in *Tools for Tomorrow* (Bruce et al., 2012). Coaching methods are especially useful for considering and assessing different options (Jones and Gorell, 2012).

Using key questions

As shown so far, the key questions cover a wide range of issues and form a broad framework to support community groups through change, whether with short-term projects or longer-term plans. These key questions are not intended as a totally comprehensive list: There are many different approaches and issues also to consider. Exploring a number of key questions with a group could take a few hours; exploring all the key questions given here with one group could take several sessions and involve research between planning sessions.

For larger support periods with the group, the material generated can form the basis of a longer-term strategic plan. For many groups this will be a useful asset for taking new opportunities and developing new ways of working. Bear in mind, the key questions are not always appropriate in the order given; for example, some groups may want to explore the changing environment before looking at their aims.

In addition to using key questions as discussed so far, there is also a wide range of organisational change methods available to use with community groups and some are referred to above (such as Bruce et al., 2012). These can be very effective, though they will usually involve more preparation in advance and more skill in using them. So, practitioners will need to consider their own levels of skill and experience in using more sophisticated methods. Different methods will have different outcomes and, as already shown above, can be used in combination with selected key questions. Bear in mind most toolkits and handbooks on organisational change are expensive to buy and designed for the private sector; much more appropriate are those designed for the community and voluntary sectors. Some examples are given in the Resources section at the end of this chapter.

So, back to the set of key questions – there are more!

➢ *Key Question H: BARRIERS – What are the barriers we face?*

A group could be clear on its aims, resources and current options but face a range of barriers that prevent it from achieving real progress. Identifying these and ways to tackle them is important. Some useful questions to ask the group are these:

➢ What are the main barriers to us achieving our aims?

➢ Are these based in the group or external?

➢ How can each one be tackled and reduced in impact?

➢ What practical steps can we now take?

➢ Who else needs to be involved?

➢ How can we empower people through the process of change?

A key issue in addressing barriers is to win hearts and minds to gain cooperation, rather than alienate people. The process of change can be threatening to some people who may need particular support and atten-tion. This support is important to help ease the acceptance of new ways of working, often involving group members, local leadership, funders or other stakeholders.

➢ *Key Question I: STAKEHOLDERS and PARTNERS – Who do we work with?*

A stakeholder can be defined as an individual or organisation that has some degree of interest in the group. Stakeholders could be funders or potential funders who have considerable influence over the group's future level of resources and security. In developing closer relationships with stakeholders, useful questions to ask the group are:

➤ How much interest does each stakeholder have in the group? For example, do they come to the group's meetings?

➤ Do they seem informed about the group's activities?

➤ How much influence does each one have?

Influence could be exercised by the stakeholder through their control of funding or their ownership of a building the group uses. If the stakeholder has a high level of influence but a low level of interest in the group, then how can the group increase the level of interest? A useful method to identify key stakeholders is called *stakeholder analysis*, where a grid can be used to plan how to build more effective relationships with a range of stakeholders (Bruce et al., 2012).

In contrast, the term *delivery partner* means an organisation that is more closely involved in the delivery of joint projects, activities and campaigns, and obviously, a stakeholder could become a delivery partner. When considering joining forces with a partner organisation, useful questions to ask the group are:

➤ What will we gain through working with this partner organisation?

➤ What will the partner organisation gain?

➤ What might we lose, or experience as problems?

➤ How can we address the problems and potential losses?

➤ How can we make the most of the benefits?

➤ How can we benefit our new partner organisation?

The stakeholder analysis method is described in www.mindtools.com/pages/article/newPPM_08.htm

➤ *Key Question J: INVOLVEMENT – How can we ensure people from different backgrounds are involved?*

In practice, the group may be excluding some members of the community in their activities. Barriers to involvement by people from minority groups can be visible, such as lack of access, or invisible, such as negative attitudes. These issues are explored further in Chapter 5. Creative use of social media can be a way to reach out to some groups; equally it can leave out others. Useful questions to use are:

> What is the spread of backgrounds of people in our group?

> How much does this reflect the local community?

> Why do the two not match?

> How can we involve more people from different backgrounds?

> What changes do we need to make in order to do this?

It is appreciated there are some groups who face discrimination and may want to meet and organise separately in order to gain confidence in a safe space. This was the case of a disability group in Leeds, who set up their own centre for people with multiple sclerosis. Equally, a lunch club set up specifically for older people would be unfairly criticised if it did not actively recruit young people to attend. However, in some cases, groups justifying excluding others by referring to 'our traditions' and 'common sense', need challenging.

Box 3.6 Involving people through social media

There are numerous ways for community groups to use social media.

Informing, involving and campaigning, for example, through:

- Setting up and maintaining a Facebook page and/or group, and through other social media, such as Twitter and Instagram.

- Regularly posting information on other organisations' Facebook pages and groups on what your community group is about, what it is doing and how to get involved. This can increase access to key decision-makers in public services and widen the reach to local groups and other stakeholders.

- Using blogging as a journal for an ongoing project or campaign.

- Live streaming meetings and events on Facebook to increase coverage.

- Using Instagram to capture and promote events through pictures, as a way to celebrate and shout about success.

- Tweeting key news and information.

▶

◀

- Using a closed Facebook group to keep your community group's members involved, up to date and contributing their own ideas to activities or campaigns.

- Organising online petitions.

- Researching what Facebook pages and groups would be best on which to post material about your activities or campaign.

Raising money:

- Using Facebook and Twitter for publicity on the need for funds.

- Using crowd-funding to raise funds for specific projects.

Consulting and engaging:

- Surveying local views to take the temperature on key issues.

- Using a WhatsApp group to provide a quick evaluation of peoples' experiences of an event, campaign or activity.

These are just examples; in practice, different social media outlets can be combined and used for different aims. Twitter is a very effective tool; it can be used for the following purposes:

- Alert key people or organisations about local issues and events by tagging them into your tweets or replying to theirs.

- Build followers over time to increase your reach.

- Use hash tags for relevant people, groups, issues or campaigns to include in your Twitter post.

- Re-tweet others' tweets to build links and exchange support.

> *Key Question K: ACCOUNTABILITY – How can we be accountable to the local community?*

Some groups remain remote from their local area or network and rarely share information on what they are doing. Useful questions to prompt action on this are:

> How do we communicate at present with our members, area or network?

> What feedback do we have on how effective this is?

> What range of media could we use to be more effective?

> What are the main things we need to communicate?

> How can this process involve new people?

➤ *Key Question L: CAMPAIGNING – How can we be effective in our campaign?*

Groups may choose to seek changes in local policies and services by carrying out a campaign to achieve certain goals. For example, in a part of inner-city Swansea, Wales, a residents' association was formed in order to improve the local environment through lobbying the Council, and its work proved very effective. It organised a campaign just before the local elections, and the campaign put them in a strong position to influence future policies on the area. In planning such a campaign, questions to ask a group are:

➤ Which issue is most important to you?

➤ What things do you wish you could change if you had the power to do so?

➤ Whom can we build relationships with, so as to work together in our campaign?

➤ What drives and motivates other groups we could work with?

➤ What talent and leadership can we draw on?

➤ How can we organise for collective public action and involvement?

These questions derive from a challenging and important book called *How to Resist: Turn Protest into Power* (Bolton, 2017). It includes the idea of carrying out a 'power analysis' where key individuals and organisations that hold power in relation to the campaign's aims are mapped and appropriate tactics identified.

Choosing key questions

As shown, there are many key questions to choose from and use, and the list can seem a bit overwhelming! As stated, some groups will only need to focus on one or two such questions. For instance, a community group could already be clear about their aims but want instead to explore new options about owning a building or starting a community enterprise. Some group members may not be interested in long-term planning or being part of group sessions, even though you have been asked to help.

Many experienced facilitators who help groups go through change use only a short list of questions, chosen carefully and worded with great skill, to unearth the underlying issues and help the group be more effective. Often just using direct and simple questions, phrased in everyday language, is very effective to cut through the baggage of other issues. It is also important not to impose questions that are inappropriate to particular groups' aims and type of activity.

Points for practitioners to consider include these:

➤ *Choosing the right question or set of questions is crucial.* With the wrong questions, a group may get lost in distractions, rather than focusing on the main problem or opportunity at hand. Careful listening by the practitioner to what is needed, and choosing appropriate questions is important.

➤ *Adapt questions as needed.* Responding to the group's own growing awareness of how to plan activities and manage change may require adding new questions during the work with them.

➤ *Keep clear notes.* Endless flip charts with words like 'development' mean very little when transcribing a week later! Ideally, type the notes the next day while your memory is still fresh. Identify in the notes what is just floated as a good idea, as opposed to a decision clearly made by the group.

➤ *Be prepared for the unexpected.* New issues may come up during the session that need to be addressed, requiring additional questions or a completely different approach not covered in this chapter.

The set of *key questions* are now continued.

➤ *Key Question M: SUPPORT – How can group members help each other through a time of change?*

Through revising its aims, identifying new options and new partner organisations to work with, the group could now be facing a process of challenging changes. It is important to recognise that emotions will be involved, rather than totally ignoring these (Hodges, 2016). Some people could feel overwhelmed by the proposed changes, seem threatened or look back to the past as a time of greater stability. Unearthing such feelings can involve risks of stirring up further tensions within the group, so any facilitation work here needs careful planning. Questions that may be useful are:

➤ How are we all feeling about the new plans?

➤ What help do you need to get involved in the changes?

➤ How can the group support you?

> *Key Question N: ACTION – How do we ensure actions are carried out?*

Many groups flounder at the point of turning good ideas into concrete plans for action. Such practical planning usually needs a set of targets to be agreed on and the resources identified to carry them out. For the longer term, this could be a two- or three-year strategy; for the short term, it may cover a few months. At worst, action plans and strategies remain hidden on computers and never get read again. To help the group to ensure implementation actually happens, useful prompt questions are:

> What are our main actions for the next few days, weeks and months?
> Given our plans, do we need any new practical arrangements?
> What regular feedback on progress do we need?
> How can we tackle blocks and barriers to achieving the changes we want?
> What do we need to do now?
> What do we need to do soon?
> What do we need to do later?
> Who will actually coordinate and lead on different actions?
> If staff are involved, how will we support them and ensure they are accountable to the group?

The terms 'Now', 'Soon' and 'Later' originate from a method called the 'Balanced Score Card', described in:

www.toolshero.com/strategy/balanced-scorecard

Another useful way to categorise proposed actions is by using traffic light colours: green – going ahead; amber – needs work on; red – not going ahead yet.

A key issue is *who* is taking the lead role in coordinating and managing the actual implementation of action plans. This needs to be decided on in order to avoid a drift into inaction or duplication. There is a big difference between having an action plan and actually carrying it out; many people confuse the two and do not recognise the differences. It is a transition where roles and responsibilities for carrying out actions need to be clarified, hopefully in a supportive manner. Practitioners can have a useful role at this point in helping groups to be clear on who is doing what and when. The W's planning tool, as described in Box 3.7, is a simple but effective system for this process. An additional element is to ensure the 'who' in each case has the support and skills they need to carry out their agreed tasks.

Box 3.7 The W's planning tool

A simple framework for short-term action planning is called the W's. Firstly, you draw up a list of actions that are now needed; then under each heading you facilitate the group's ideas on:

- What – describing the action needed
- When by – date for completion, key milestones
- Who – who is leading, who is helping, who is being consulted
- Where – location, if appropriate
- With – resources needed
- Why – how does this address our aims?

Such planning methods can be very effective, though are usually concerned with the short term.

➤ *Key Question O: EVALUATION – How do we assess our effectiveness in achieving our aims?*

The evaluation of short or long-term plans should be considered at an early stage and not just be an add-on at the end. Useful questions for the group to consider are:

➤ How will we assess our effectiveness in achieving our aims?

➤ How will we know the impact our group has had?

➤ What information will we need to collect to do this?

➤ What indicators can we use for success?

➤ When are useful points in our plans for the evaluation of progress?

➤ Who do we involve in assessing our success?

➤ How can we learn from our experience to do an even better job next time?

The effort spent on such evaluations needs to be proportional to the scale of the initiative. A small-scale project, such as organising a summer festival, would not need as many resources and time spent on evaluation compared to, say, a three-year programme of a group's work. For smaller-scale projects and activities, a facilitated review session, looking at what went well and what could be improved next time, could be all that is needed. An excellent approach to evaluation is called LEAP, as described in Box 3.8. Chanan gives a useful introduction to evaluation in Twelvetrees (2017, p. 48).

Box 3.8 LEAP: a planning and learning framework

LEAP stands for learning, evaluation and planning.

It helps communities to identify the difference they hope to make, to plan more effectively, work in partnership and learn the lessons from their experience. The LEAP framework can be used in different contexts; to support the work of different sectors; and at project, programme and policy level. The five key stages of LEAP are:

- Step 1: What difference do we want to make?

- Step 2: How will we know we made a difference?

- Step 3: How will we go about making the difference? What resources will we use? What methods will we use? In what ways will we use them?

- Step 4: How are we making sure it is happening?

- Step 5: Have we made the difference? What are the lessons we have learned? What will we need to do now?

The five stages are presented as a cycle. It is particularly useful as a tool to support partnership working and local community planning. LEAP also uses the terms outcomes and outputs, which are very useful for evaluation: *Outcomes* are the differences that are intended to result from a given activity. *Outputs* are the actions taken or services delivered to achieve the outcomes. In other words, outputs are the means of achieving outcomes; for example, outputs could be 20 people completing a training course on leadership, and the outcome would be to create well-informed community leaders, able to use their knowledge of community needs in a skilful and accountable manner.

(Adapted from Barr and Dailly, 2006)

Concluding points

As mentioned, the range of key questions needs to be used with creativity and good listening – their use needs to be selective and tailor made, based on the group's needs and the brief agreed with them. Participating in sessions with a facilitator using key questions can be an empowering experience, both for individual group members and the group as a whole. Helping groups to achieve their own set of aims will also be an empowering experience, and taking stock early on in the process can build confidence and strengthen the group's bonds. Identifying resources and stakeholder relationships helps group members to value existing organisational strengths. Overall, effective facilitation can help individual groups to work more effectively towards their aims and build a sense of achievement. In these different ways, the process of building organisations can be an empowering experience for community groups.

As well as working with individual groups, community empowerment can involve supporting a number of groups across an area, as described in 'community strengths profiles' which are now discussed.

Box 3.9 How *not* to carry out facilitation work with community groups

Here are some helpful hints on what you should not do:

- Decide on their problem even before you have met the group.
- Use lots of unexplained jargon about 'organisational structures' and 'outcome indicators' that no one can understand.
- Turn up late for the session in a state of panic.
- Use the same facilitation methods you always use, irrespective of what the group really needs.
- Try to impose your views as much as possible.
- Don't bother with a brief, and keep your role unclear.
- Break confidentiality by sharing any juicy gossip with other groups.
- Spend ages writing the final report and send it to them six months late.
- Don't evaluate your work in any way.
- In your write-up, describe the group's experience as empowering for them, even without asking them if it was.
- Do exactly the same the next time.

Part Two: working collectively

Part Two looks at ways to support groups collectively in an area or network, rather than just individually as discussed so far. Bringing community groups together in events, forums and networks has many advantages and will contribute towards building stronger communities. Networking is explored in Chapter 4. After a brief review of a selection of approaches to community profiling, Part Two focuses on a community strengths profiling method to collectively support community groups.

Community profiles

There are many different approaches to area profiles and mapping, such as village plans, neighbourhood plans and asset mapping. Each has a different focus:

> *Neighbourhood planning.* This involves mapping the different types of land use in an area. Based on the Localism Act of 2011, it gives communities in England opportunities to develop a vision for their neighbourhood and choose where they want new homes, shops and offices to be built, what they look like and what infrastructure should be provided.

> *Community-led planning.* This is important for rural communities. It can take the form of a parish plan or a community or village design statement. The ACRE Network (www.acre.org.uk) provides resources to communities so that they can produce high-quality plans that meet the needs of all members of the community.

> *Assessment of the level of resident activity.* This could map the level of individual resident activity in a neighbourhood. Health authorities may be interested in identifying a link between increased resident activity and improved health. Indicators are available to assist such mapping, though more research is needed (Chanan and Fisher, 2017). Such an assessment could also include information on how easy or hard it is for residents to start new groups and find the ones that exist.

> *Long-term review of community groups.* Over time, are groups in decline and closing down? Are new groups starting up? This would be a review of an area over, say, a five-year period, not just the current profile of groups.

> *Social indicators profile.* These usually focus on statistical data on major social indicators of health, crime levels, school achievement and so on.

> *Asset mapping.* These often focus on resources, such as parks, and available public buildings and local skills as well as the range of community groups and institutions. See Box 3.10 for two interesting examples.

Box 3.10 Community building in the US – and asset mapping in South Africa

Community building is a particular version of asset-based community development, involving a number of key stages (Kretzmann and McKnight, 1993). The process often starts by drawing up a map of local assets, focusing on the gifts, skills and

▶

◀

capacities of residents, as well as the resources and activities of local groups. The inventory includes land and available buildings, as well as resources in the local economy. The approach is also about linking together community groups to increase their power and solve problems. 'Local institutions' are then identified in the mapping stage, by which the authors mean, for example, public services, local religious groups, libraries, colleges, voluntary organisations and businesses located in the community. The community-building process involves developing relationships between residents, local groups and institutions, based on the strengths and capacities of all parties involved. This process includes outreach, for example, to older people, young people and people with disabilities. Community building also involves bringing together a broadly representative group to build a community vision and gather resources from external organisations to support the locally defined initiatives.

The asset-based, self-help approach described by Kretzmann and McKnight is inspiring in how it involves the grass roots, and commendable in that it actively encourages the inclusion of different parts of the community. However, the approach raises several points of concern. Firstly, there is a practical question, about who actually undertakes the extensive work involved in the mapping exercise. Identifying local skills and actually helping people to make use of them in a meaningful and useful way is very time intensive; if it is not followed through with some activities fairly quickly after the initial contact, it can raise expectations and then disappoint people. A second concern is about the order of the stages; it appears that only after the mapping exercise has been carried out are community leaders brought together to discuss priorities and a future plan (Kretzmann and McKnight, 1993, p. 351). Could it be the other way around, with the community itself at an early stage deciding if asset mapping is appropriate as a current priority and, if so, taking the lead in its design and implementation?

Asset Mapping in Thekwana, South Africa

Thekwana is part of the Potemfi group of villages that fall within the Royal Bafokeng Nation. A workshop was held in the village, based in a local church, from Monday to Friday, 27–31 May 2013, and included an asset mapping process. The workshop was facilitated by an organisation called Space 4 Impact, with help from other local groups, in order to involve residents in improving life in the village.

The workshop started with a 'Trans Act Walk' on the Monday. The participants were divided into two groups, each mapping out the historical timeline of the village and its people and how life had transformed from when the village was established. This was an interactive session within each group, followed by a sharing of information. Because there was a generational mix of older, middle-aged and young people, this exercise had a profound effect on the participants who learnt about the history of the village through story telling. The workshop also involved social observations highlighting the problems of crime, prostitution and gangsterism. A resident drew cartoons that showed the crime observations and possible solutions.

The asset mapping process itself identified a range of assets in the village. Human assets or 'gifts' included those of the 'head', such as literacy, problem solving, money

▶

management, business and trading, and accounting. Assets of the 'heart' included compassion, care of the elderly, sense of humour, conflict resolution, willingness to collaborate, and cooperative spirit, and those of the 'hands' included carpentry, farming, cooking, mechanics, sewing, weaving, and animal husbandry. The group discovered that one of the men was a beauty therapist, that an elderly woman taught dance lessons, and that many people could drive, cook and sing, and some of the group had businesses.

The participants also broke up into three groups and mapped out the social assets that included associations, including churches, Stokvels, burial societies, political parties, sports associations and businesses.

As well as looking at assets based in the infrastructure and the local environment, the workshop also explored the flows inwards and outwards of money, using information relating to the number of households, population and other statistics available.

Thirty-two participants completed the workshop, with two opposing groups making great strides to work together. It led to a new understanding of the lack of skills in the village and how by obtaining these skills, projects could become successful. Most of the future projects identified were large projects and during the following few months mentoring programmes were set up so that the various leaders in the village could realistically pick their team in order to implement the projects.

Community strengths profiles

A different form of profiling from those described so far is called a *community strengths profile*. Such a profile describes particular features of community groups across an area, such as their aims and achievements, the way they are organised, any funding and resources they have, as well as any training and support they are already getting. The findings can identify the *level of community organisation* across a whole village or neighbourhood and be used to plan capacity-building initiatives. The process of creating the profile itself can enable groups to think more about where they are going and what their development needs might be. This method focuses on groups, rather than on individuals; community strengths profiles have been carried out by a range of communities across the UK and are being actively supported in Scotland. The community strengths profile method was originally developed in Bradford (Skinner and Wilson, 2002) and further developed by the Scottish Community Development Centre.

An essential starting point in devising a community strengths profile is to involve local groups to discuss the idea and only proceed if they give their support. The profiling then involves two surveys. One is a survey of local community groups, which usually requires some outreach work to ensure a wide range of groups is included. The second survey is of larger organisations based in or around the area that are providing or can provide capacity-building support to those groups. A key element of a community strengths profile is that by carrying out two surveys, it looks at both the *level of organisation* at the grass roots, as well as the *level of support* available to groups in the area. In combination, these two elements can build a comprehensive picture of existing community strengths and inform an action plan for the way forward.

Local groups can be fully involved in carrying out the surveys, for example by helping to build the list of groups and providing volunteers to visit them. The groups survey can help to build local links and stimulate thinking about the area's development needs. Once the two surveys are completed, the main data findings can be presented at an open workshop session where local groups then take the lead in deciding the way forward. The community strengths profile could be an independent initiative or part of an existing local regeneration or village plan. Community strengths assessments are a systematic way to identify needs and strengths of groups in neighbourhoods. The method can also be adapted to use with network-based groups, such as disability groups across a city region. For a well-designed toolkit, published by the Scottish Community Development Centre, see the Resources section at the end of this publication.

Box 3.11 Strengthening Communities in West Lothian

In 2011, the Local Authority, in partnership with the West Lothian Regeneration Team, developed a local strategy for strengthening communities in Livingston. Working with representatives from community learning, health improvement, tenants' groups and voluntary organisations, they organised a survey of community groups and the support available to them. They found more than 100 groups in the Livingston area of 63,000 people. Through workshops and publicity, 23 questionnaires were completed by local groups.

The data were analysed using the four key themes of building skills, building organisations, building equality and building involvement. This assessment stage was carried out through a workshop involving local groups, using the Building Stronger Communities toolkit materials; see link below. A second workshop focused on the survey of agencies in the area providing training and support for local groups. The two sets of findings were then combined to inform the development of a strategy for community capacity building. The Building Stronger Communities toolkit is available from www.scdc.org.uk.

This type of assessment can give a systematic description of the baseline of community strengths by focusing on the needs and strengths of community and voluntary groups. It involves the following elements:

➢ *Preparation.* Consult local groups to ensure they support the idea of producing a community strengths profile. Identify the range of groups in the neighbourhood; this may involve some outreach work to ensure any existing list is comprehensive and inclusive, especially of minority groups.

➢ *Survey of local community groups.* This can use a range of questions. Such questions could cover size of each group, their aims and plans, their resources and partnerships, how they are organised and what, if any, training and advice they already access.

➢ *Survey of organisations providing support.* This requires identifying which organisations are available to provide organisational support for local groups. A community strengths profile carried out in inner-city Bradford identified 22 such different agencies and organisations. This second survey builds a picture of the level of support in an area and could include the council, other public service providers, the larger voluntary organisations, trusts and charities.

➢ *Review.* The information from the two surveys is gathered together and key findings shared at a workshop. All local groups should be invited to the workshop, as well as those support organisations that completed the second survey. Based on the data gathered, participants are invited to give their views on the state of health of local groups, using a simple voting method. The pattern of voting is then used to identify *the level of community organisation*, based on the four key themes for strengthening communities.

➢ *Action plan.* An action plan involving local groups and support organisations, describing key changes needed, is drawn up.

Box 3.12 Examples of survey questions

The survey of local community groups in the strengths profile can be designed to reflect the four themes for strengthening communities introduced in Chapter 1, as repeated below. It could include questions based on the four themes, such as the following:

Building Organisations

Does the group have a clear set of aims?

To what extent do their members feel they are achieving their aims?

▶

◀

To what extent do they have resources they need?

Are they dependent on grants?

What are their other forms of income, if any?

Do they receive any advice or organisational support?

Building People

Does the group ever identify its members' learning needs?

Do group members participate in learning activities?

Are learning opportunities available that match what the group needs?

What barriers do group members experience to taking up learning opportunities?

Building Involvement

What range of activities is the group involved in?

Does the group feel they are involving enough people?

Does the group influence decision-making about its community?

Building Equality

Does the group involve people from different backgrounds?

Does the group have any policies or guidelines on equal opportunities?

Does the group include people from minorities?

Do members challenge discrimination?

The questions above are not written with the precise wording to be used in a survey questionnaire for groups but are included here to describe the range of issues such questions could cover. Questions for the actual survey need to be written in ways that do not overload the group member completing the questionnaire form and must avoid using jargon wherever possible.

Summary

Chapter 3 has covered some practical material on supporting groups through growth and change. It looked at:

➤ Ways to help groups to identify their needs and strengths

➤ A series of key questions to facilitate effective change

➤ Community strengths profiles as a way to identify the needs of community groups across a geographical area.

Key points of this chapter have been:

- ➤ Change in groups needs to originate from the group and not be imposed upon them.

- ➤ A facilitation approach to supporting groups can contribute to members feeling empowered through a process of change.

- ➤ A set of key questions can be useful for facilitating organisational change in groups, although they need to be chosen carefully, based on an assessment of the group's needs and strengths.

- ➤ Community strengths profiles are useful to build a wider picture of both the levels of organisation and levels of support.

In terms of the definition of stronger communities introduced in Chapter 1, building organisations will contribute to developing communities that, in particular, are *active* and *organised*. Working collectively with a number of groups will also contribute to communities being better *connected*.

Developing your practice

Using the key questions with groups can seem daunting if you are not familiar with this field of work. Some useful practical points are:

- ➤ *Build up your confidence and skills in stages* – Start with a small piece of work with a group you already know.

- ➤ *Work with others* – Learn skills through co-facilitation with other people who have more experience.

- ➤ *Check your brief* – Ensure your support is based on what the group explicitly wants, not doing the same thing you did last time.

- ➤ *Minimise your risks* – If you think a particular set of questions or methods will be too challenging for a group or for your skill level, it may be best not to use it.

- ➤ *Get feedback* – Obtain feedback both from colleagues and from the group on how your support could have been improved.

You need to be responsible for your own work with groups. This book can only act as an introduction to using different approaches; it is not a comprehensive training manual or handbook. You may need to build your skills to be able to use them effectively; in particular, helping groups to develop a longer-term strategy needs a good understanding of organisational planning issues (Johnson et al., 2009).

Related issues to consider in your work as a practitioner with groups are:

➢ What requests for help from groups will you accept, and which might you turn down?

➢ How would you identify the type of help needed?

➢ What would you do if a group asked for a type of help that went against your values (for example, asking for help to run a building that excluded certain members of the local community)?

➢ If a group chose an option for the future that you really thought was a mistake, how would you respond?

➢ Would a community strengths profile be useful in your neighbourhood?

➢ What values will underlie your work as a community practitioner?

➢ How will your support be an empowering experience for the group?

Resources

www.scdc.org.uk/media/resources/BSC/Building%20Stronger%20Communties.pdf
Tools for Tomorrow is available on www.ncvo.org.uk
Building Stronger Communities practical assessment and planning tool for community capacity building is available on www.scdc.org.uk
www.scdc.org.uk/media/resources/documents/LEAP%20Step-By-Step.pdf
www.betterevaluation.org/en
www.evaluationtoolbox.net.au/
www.knowhownonprofit.org/organisation/operations
www.toolshero.com/strategy/balanced-scorecard/
www.cass.city.ac.uk/faculties-and-research/centres/cce/resources/tools-for-success
www.data.ncvo.org.uk/a/almanac16/a-focus-on-small-charities
www.healthempowerment.co.uk
www.acre.org.uk/rural-issues/community-planning
www.healthempowerment.co.uk/wp-content/uploads/2018/01/COMMISSIONING-CD-FOR-HEALTH-C4CC-2018-1.pdf
www.birmingham.ac.uk/generic/tsrc/research/below-the-radar/index.aspx

References: Chapter 3

Barr, A. and Dailly, J. (2006) *LEAP Step by Step*. London: Community Development Foundation.
Blake, I. and Bush, C. (2009) *Project Managing Change*. Harlow: Prentice Hall.

Bolton, M. (2017) *How to Resist: Turn Protest into Power.* London: Bloomsbury.

Bruce, I., Copeman, C., Forrest, A., Lesirge, R., Palmer, P. and Patel, A. (2012) *Tools for Tomorrow.* London: NCVO.

Burns, P. (2011) *Entrepreneurship and Small Business: Start-Up, Growth and Maturity.* London: Red Globe Press.

Chanan, G. and Fisher, B. (2017) *Commissioning Community Development for Health: A Concise Handbook.* London: Coalition for Collaborative Care and the Health Empowerment Leverage Project (HELP).

Copeman, C. and Griffith Gray, M. (2009) *Looking Out.* London: National Council for Voluntary Organisations (NCVO).

Gilchrist, A. (2007) *Equalities and Communities.* London: Community Development Foundation.

Hayes, J. (2010) *The Theory and Practice of Change Management.* London: Red Globe Press.

Hodges, J. (2016) *Managing and Leading People through Organisational Change.* London: Kogan Page.

Johnson, G., Scholes, K. and Whittington, R. (2009) *Fundamentals of Strategy.* Harlow: Prentice Hill.

Jones, G. and Gorell, R. (2012) *50 Top Tools for Coaching.* London: Kogan Page.

Kretzmann, J. and McKnight, J. (1993) *Building Communities from the Inside Out.* Skokie: ACTA Publications

Mullins, L.J. (1993) *Management and Organisational Behaviour.* London: Pitman.

NCVO. (2016) *U.K. Civic Society Almanac.* London: NCVO.

Paton, R. and McCalman, J. (2000) *Change Management: A Guide to Effective Implementation.* London: Sage Publications.

Phillimore, J., McCabe, A., Proctor, A.S. and Taylor, R. (2010) *Understanding the Distinctiveness of Small Scale, Third Sector Activity: The Role of Local Knowledge and Networks in Shaping Below the Radar Actions* Working Paper 33. Birmingham: Third Sector Research Centre.

Skinner, S. and Wilson, M. (2002) *Assessing Community Strengths.* London: The Community Development Foundation.

Twelvetrees, A. (2017) *Community Development, Social Action and Social Planning.* London: Red Globe Press.

4

Building Involvement

Chapter 2 was about building people; Chapter 3 focused on supporting local organisations. This chapter looks at how people and community organisations can have more influence on decisions that affect them. It also explores how communities can get more involved in activities to improve the quality of life at local level. The process of *building involvement* will contribute to creating more *active* and *participative* communities, two of the seven key features used in the definition of 'strong communities'.

A first question to look at is: How can the level of influence over local decisions be strengthened at the grass roots? In the UK, modern democracy is characterised by low voter turnout for local elections, with some residents turning to other forms of community action and protest, such as environmental campaigns. People often want to contribute to decisions that affect their lives and their community but feel alienated and left out; this chapter explores how communities can have more influence.

A second question to look at is: How can the level of involvement be strengthened at the grass roots? Around half of the population of the UK is a member of an organisation, with sports clubs being the most popular type of membership organisation. Millions of people are also involved in community activity, in supporting their neighbours, and are helping to organise events and run local activities. For example, every year volunteers in Wales contribute 221 million hours of voluntary activity (WCVA, 2017). More than one in four people formally volunteer once a month and about one-fifth of the UK population is involved in social action in their local community (Hornung et al., 2017). This bedrock of relationships and collective activity can be described as 'social capital' (Putman, 2000), in particular, involving 'bonds' and 'bridges' between people to provide a platform for social support (HM Treasury, 2005).

Using a 'Wheel of Participation' as a framework, this chapter addresses these two key questions: How can the level of influence over local decisions be strengthened at the grass roots, and how can the level of involvement can be strengthened at the grass roots?

In this chapter, the term *involvement* is used to mean people getting involved in community activities and groups, and the term *participation* to mean individuals and groups engaging with service providers and other authorities to influence decisions. However, in practice there is often overlap between the two. In this book the title *Building Involvement* is used as a short-hand term to refer to both *involvement* and *participation*. *Building involvement* is a means to an end, contributing to the building of stronger communities, as described in Chapter 1.

The Wheel of Participation

One way to describe the rich diversity of involvement and participation that exists in communities is to use the image of a wheel. A 'Wheel of Participa-tion' presented here includes six main pathways for involvement and par-ticipation and is based visually on the spokes of the Wheel. The Wheel can be used to help *individuals* look at the kind of community activities they could get involved in. However, the main aim of the Wheel is to help *com-munity groups* make informed choices about their priorities and activities, in order to achieve their aims. Practitioners can also use the Wheel to help groups review ways in which they can have more influence. Any one group might be involved in one, two or more pathways; there is no assumption that they should be involved in all or most of them. The six main pathways in the Wheel of Participation are shown in Box 4.1:

Box 4.1 The Wheel of Participation

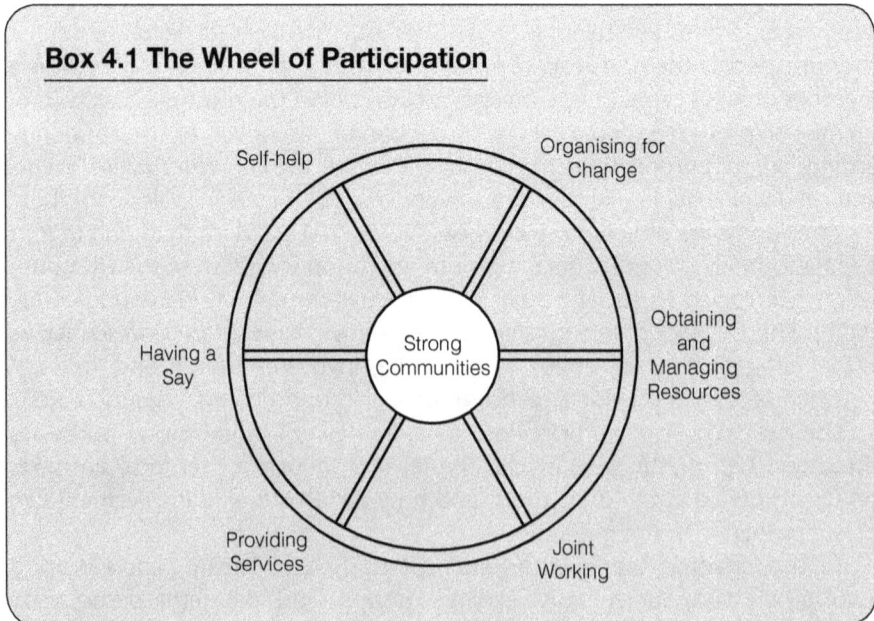

Self-help

Organising for Change

Having a Say

Strong Communities

Obtaining and Managing Resources

Providing Services

Joint Working

These six options for community involvement and participation, visually described as pathways on a wheel, offer a range of choices for action and influence. Some of the six pathways primarily involve *individuals* as residents, volunteers or service users, while others involve a *collective* activity; however, in practice, there is often no clear dividing line between the two. Some community groups may be involved in only one or two pathways, such as 'Self-help' and 'Obtaining and Managing Resources'; others may be actively involved in a much wider range of options. The levels of activity will vary between pathways for different groups and there is no expectation, in any way, that groups should be involved in all six pathways. There will often be some overlap between the activities involved in the different pathways; obtaining and managing resources, for example, may be an essential part of several other options. However, having an awareness of each underlying *function* is useful for community groups when setting priorities and planning activities.

With these six main pathways, the Wheel can be a useful framework for understanding the process of strengthening communities, focusing here on increasing the levels of community involvement and influence.

Box 4.2 Introducing the Wheel of Participation

Here is a fictitious example to demonstrate how the pathways on the Wheel offer contrasting ways in which communities can participate. A popular community centre has been funded by the Local Authority for several years, with a wide range of activities and services provided to the local area. The cuts in the Council's leisure services budget now mean the centre could close in six months' time. Local groups who use the centre are considering a range of choices:

- *Self-help* – Local community groups, without any financial help from the Council, pool their resources and time to run the place on their own.

- *Organising for Change* – Residents campaign to keep the centre open, and, in order to do so, join up with other campaigning groups.

- *Obtaining and Managing Resources* – This could involve local groups applying for funding from trusts in order to keep the centre going.

- *Joint Working* – This could mean the Council providing building maintenance and insurance, while local groups run the place by providing volunteers.

- *Providing Services* – The centre's management committee gets a contract from the Council to provide adult social care support, based in the building.

- *Having A Say* – This could mean members of local groups attending a council-run consultation meeting and expressing their views on the centre's future.

The six pathways

The six pathways are now explored in more detail and how the Wheel of Participation can be used with community groups is then discussed.

Self-help

This includes a wide range of small-scale, often unfunded local activities, organised and run by volunteers and community groups. Self-help can include activities such as starting luncheon clubs, running bingo sessions, organising environmental clean-ups and running community festivals. Some self-help activities can be mainly for the benefit of members of a defined group, such as a walking group, whereas others may provide benefits for the wider community, such as a 'Friends of the Park' group. Often, in such settings, people get involved as informal volunteers, through local contacts, as opposed to the more structured system of volunteering where people are introduced and supported through a local volunteer centre. Self-help activities occur widely across the UK and provide valuable forms of social capital.

In Blackburn, Lancashire, a small community centre runs a range of activities, including bingo sessions one morning per week. The centre has a homely feel, with its own resident cat! Apart from being a lot of fun, the centre brings people together and helps reduce loneliness in a deprived neighbourhood.

In Todmorden in West Yorkshire, local residents took action to improve their town environment by planting vegetables on unused areas of land to provide food for poor families. The scheme, called Incredible Edible, has been very successful, and similar schemes are now established around the UK.

Self-help might involve some assistance from external sources, but it is mostly about do-it-yourself community action. In terms of influence, self-help can give communities more control over the activities they are directly involved in. Larger scale self-help initiatives involve what can be called 'projects', such as housing projects or energy production schemes, requiring access to external funds and technical expertise. However, whatever the scale, the emphasis is on people doing things themselves. Self-help has been promoted as the key solution to local problems, especially in some deprived areas, and, as a specific approach, has a long history. It has been especially significant in poorer countries, where local people have become disillusioned about relying on elected bodies and external authorities to tackle their problems and, having no alternative, have taken action to do things themselves. Self-help is an effective way to involve people at local level. However, there are wider issues about promoting self-help as a strategy in deprived communities; if communities are solving their own problems, will it imply less outside help is needed? Some commentators argue that focusing on the promotion of self-help and using local assets does not imply that such areas do not require external support (Kretzmann and McKnight,1993). However, the main focus of such dedicated self-help schemes seems to be people being asked to solve their own problems, rather than mobilising people to change local policies and priorities or access resources from other sources. The pathways on the Wheel of Participation can be a useful prompt here for communities to consider questions such as the following: Is our first priority self-help, or organising a campaign to obtain more resources from outside the area?

Organising for Change

This approach is about communities taking a stand about issues that affect them, such as running a campaign against cuts in public services or about pollution caused by a local factory. It can include residents organising online networks to engage in protests, or involve people uniting against racism. Compared to 'Self-help', 'Organising for Change' is often a more confrontational approach. In some cases, residents may resort to 'Organising for Change' as a strategy after 'Having a Say' or 'Self-help' has, in their eyes, not addressed the issue enough or has led to nothing. It may include organising local networks to engage in protests.

For example, after the tragic fire on the 14th of June, 2017 in north Kensington, when 92 people died, the Grenfell Tower block residents have been involved in a campaign to be allocated proper, alternative accommodation. Another example of locally based action is Botley, a town just west of Oxford, where residents organised a successful campaign to save and improve their town centre. Botley had a run-down 1970s' style shopping centre and offices that needed redevelopment. Developers proposed also demolishing an interesting 1930s shopping parade, a large sheltered housing centre and the local vicarage, to build a large eight-storey development. Several politicians backed the idea and the Council's planning service recommended approval, but 18 months later the Planning Committee unanimously rejected it. This reversal occurred because local people had got organised. The campaign involved a survey of public support, some well-run public meetings, lots of letter writing and detailed briefings for councillors. Central to their success were some colourful demonstrations, some with over 800 people, and work with the local MP. It was an imaginative approach to campaigning, with one resident writing a pantomime about it all. The original proposal was eventually replaced by a much smaller development, more acceptable to local residents.

Through campaigning, publicity, mobilising and similar activities, communities can build movements and networks to challenge public authorities and large companies. For example, TELCO (The East London Citizens Organisation) has been active for over 20 years with community organising and social justice campaigns to improve living standards. This has included campaigning for increased employment opportunities, higher wages and affordable housing schemes. At national level, Citizens UK has a history of successful campaigns; their approach includes building good working relationships with key decision-makers, such as MPs. Such large-scale campaigning is very effective, but usually requires the focused organisation of a large number of people and institutions and is not a readily available option for small-scale community groups.

Box 4.3 Using social media for campaigns

In using social media for locally based community campaigns, it is worth doing a risk assessment at an early stage. Some dos and don'ts to consider are the following:

- *Public disclosure of incorrect information* – It is vital to ensure all information being distributed via social media postings is accurate.

- *Insufficient information leading to complaints* – The right level of information needs to be given.

- *Poor use of settings or permissions* – If groups are not accustomed to using a social media platform, it is best they get advice on settings and permissions, for example in relation to privacy.

- *Consistency* – Members of community groups need to take care to avoid expressing personal views in the name of the whole organisation.

- *Personal comments* – Comments directed at individuals, such as staff in public sector organisations, should be avoided.

There is a big issue in resourcing a social media presence, too – planning stories, sequencing, thinking about writing styles, editing, accuracy of information, and the use of photos. This is a job in itself, and building a presence requires a regular, planned, drip-feed of posting stories and news, with both tagging and following on Twitter.

The HB Mama Dread's Masqueraders, a Leeds-based carnival troupe, use social media to communicate, campaign and generate interest in their troupe. Using social media also helps generate a culture of self-help and enthusiasm amongst its members. Facebook and Twitter are part of their public face, explaining the troupe's work commitment to social change and their creative responses to issues of the day.

Obtaining and managing resources

This pathway is about communities obtaining grants, buildings, funding for staff and other assets and gaining access to equipment, office and meeting space. In terms of influence, where community organisations obtain grants, run buildings and generally build up their physical assets, they will probably have greater influence on their immediate environment. For example, in Stretford, near Manchester, Stretford Public Hall was transferred to the community from the local council, which led to an energetic programme of community-run activities. The Friends of Stretford Public Hall, a charitable body, was formed in 2014 to take on the ownership and running of the building for the benefit of the community. It is an inspiring initiative – people involved feel they have a high level of influence over a major community resource.

Obtaining local buildings for community use, such as through an asset transfer scheme run by the local authority, can create many different ways for communities to get involved and have direct control over their own centre. Asset transfer is where the council gifts a building to a local group or rents it to them at a 'pepper-corn' rent level. However, in some cases, asset transfer has meant a community group inheriting a building with demanding maintenance problems and consequently becoming inward-looking due to the new responsibilities of paying the bills, with little outside support.

'Obtaining and Managing Resources' can provide a range of opportunities for community involvement but needs care in how it is carried out. Local fund-raising initiatives, such as a sponsored walk to raise money for a community group, can build new relationships and create good publicity opportunities. Fund-raising through grant applications is another useful source of obtaining resources, but the demanding process of making grant applications may not be the best way to get people involved.

An inspiring example of a participative approach to fund-raising is in Holywell Green, West Yorkshire, where residents reacted to the threatened closure of the Holywell Inn village pub by setting up a scheme to buy the property. The pub was the only one left in the village and the aim has been to convert it into a community hub. The residents set up the Holywell Community Pub Limited, a not-for-profit Community Benefit Society, and issued a share offer at £25 per person per month to initially raise £120,000. The Society has also been organising fund-raising events, such as an annual music festival and other community activities. As well as being based on the main site, the festival also involves outreach work in care homes, a special school and a hospice.

Joint working

'Joint Working' is another major option for communities to get involved and have local influence. This could be, for example, where community groups join forces with a public sector organisation to run a youth project or improve a neglected park. Local partnerships, where a range of organisations work together to improve the area, are also examples. Joint Working provides opportunities for representatives from community organisations to work alongside public services and local companies on joint projects, providing opportunities to inform and influence decisions at planning and delivery stages.

Joint Working can be short term, focusing on delivering a particular project, or longer term, where a partnership body is established. To work effectively, it needs a degree of trust between the different parties involved and a shared set of aims and values. Joint Working needs effective leadership and facilitation, so that meetings are focused, participants are willing to share relevant information and community representatives are accountable to their group or network. However, some groups have felt their contribution in joint working with public services has been undervalued and that they are not fully involved in decision-making (Twelvetrees, 2017).

The term 'co-production' has been increasingly popular over the last two decades. As an approach, it is more than joint design and delivery of services with communities by the public sector. It is based on the principle that public service providers can perceive communities and service users as assets who have skills and resources. The approach is about mutual support and building reciprocity, involving community networks and local organisations. Put in another way, the principles of co-production include valuing the role families and groups play in contributing to well-being, building social networks and facilitating strong, enduring relationships. Through co-production, public organisations need to adopt new ways of relating to 'clients' and service users, providing opportunities for personal growth and development to people, so that they are treated as assets, not burdens (Cahn, 2000).

Examples of joint working come from Northern Ireland, described in Box 4.4, and Blackpool, described in Box 4.5.

Box 4.4 Joint working on a housing initiative in Northern Ireland

The Doury Road Community Association is based in an estate in Ballymena in County Antrim. It is a working-class Protestant estate and was suffering from neglect and lack of investment. Through joint working with the Northern Ireland Housing Executive, and support from the Community Foundation of Northern Ireland (CFNI), the area went through a major process of renovation.

Originally, the area had been a social housing estate of over 500 houses, with a settled community. Subsequently, many people had bought their houses under a homesteading scheme, where Northern Ireland Housing Executive tenants could purchase their homes at reduced rates, based on the amount of time they had been tenants. The unforeseen consequences arising from this were that many people took up this opportunity and then sold their properties. This, in itself, was not an issue, but private landlords became active in the area and bought as many of these properties as they could. The properties were then rented out.

Heroin and other drugs landed into Ballymena at the same time this was going on, since many of the properties for rent were rented by drug dealers. The area became rundown, and drugs took hold within the community. Many of the drug dealers then left the properties and these fell into disrepair. Families left the area, and their Housing Executive houses were left abandoned as well. The Housing Executive had no one on the waiting list for this area, and whole streets were boarded up and left derelict. The more rundown the area became, the more people left, until entire streets were abandoned and only 140 out of 500 properties were occupied. The Housing Executive were knocking down streets but without a cohesive approach, and the area included patches of waste ground. Some people from ethnic minorities living in the wider Ballymena area were becoming victims of racism and hate crimes, and many were forced to move out of their homes.

CFNI came into the area with their 'Communities in Transition' project and helped to start a local residents' group that became the Doury Road Community Association. Despite the area being blighted by drugs, poverty and a lack of statutory engagement, the community wanted to regenerate their area. Though it took a while for agencies to get around the table and work with residents, key things were done to regenerate the area:

- The Housing Executive agreed to refurbish some of the houses.

- The residents' group found out who some of the private landlords were and persuaded them to do up their properties. In turn, the group offered to find them tenants who would look after their properties.

- The group approached families that had moved out and encouraged some of them to come back and buy into the regeneration programme.

- The group approached the Ballymena Minority Ethnic Forum and the Housing Executive with a plan to address racism in the area. They created a welcome pack in several languages for people from ethnic minorities.

- The group worked to assure minorities of a welcome and safe place to live, having done preparatory work with the existing residents around this.

Through joint working, led by the community association, the initiative has been a success. The area is improving, and new families have now moved in.

Box 4.5 Joint working on an arts project in Blackpool

LeftCoast, an independent arts organisation, and the Arts Council's Creative People and Places project, were invited to work in the Mereside area of Blackpool by a local housing association called Blackpool Coastal Housing, and Better Start, a partnership looking at early years provision across Blackpool. The initial aim was to investigate how the green spaces on Mereside could be redeveloped, working with the local community and artists to creatively reimagine that space. Whilst changes to the green space did undoubtedly happen, one of the most powerful and unplanned outcomes was the bringing together of a group of mainly female residents who wanted to see action in the place where they lived. Called Mereside and Friends in Action (MAFIA), they were formed through an shared interest in making their estate a more interesting place to live, providing opportunities for their children and a general passion for the wider community. Inspired by visits to other places, such as Liverpool and the Granby project, the group gained the confidence to ask how they could achieve something similar on Mereside.

Various activities were developed including a community orchard, a multi-use games area, and a creative holiday activity programme. In terms of joint working, an interesting partnership developed between MAFIA and the police. Directly opposite the Mereside estate, the police were developing a piece of land for the new North West division headquarters. Concerns about the new building that would overlook the estate were understandably high. With LeftCoast as a facilitator, the Police and Crime Commissioner decided to put some money into arts commissioning, in partnership with the group. Although MAFIA members had many skills, they had not until this point directly commissioned an artist to create a public artwork. So, with their involvement, LeftCoast supported a co-commissioning model between the police, the community, the Police and Crime Commissioner and the construction company. An open brief was written, and the commissioning panel went through a selection process to commission artist Andrew Small. This was an exercise in trust, and pushing the boundaries; they chose an artist who valued the process and who could not tell them exactly what the artwork would be.

Titled *We All Make Mistakes*, the neon light work is situated on the outside wall of the headquarters to engage all who visit. The work is made up of neon windmill sails that are representative of the iconic Mereside Windmill that the community identifies as a landmark. If the community was to have a badge, this would be it. The sails turn at varying speeds to represent the work going on inside the headquarters and the amount of calls received. It may appear that the building does not change from one day to the next, but behind these walls are the inner workings of a police force who are responding to the community's needs. This work of art seeks to merge both worlds, inextricably linked as they are; the community that live surrounding the headquarters and the community of police who have moved into the building.

Providing services

Many large voluntary organisations already provide a range of valuable services to their communities, either locally or over a large geographical area. These are sometimes based on contracts with a public body, such as the Local Authority or Clinical Commissioning Group, and are usually valuable contributions to the quality of life of users and communities. The advantage of this arrangement for the public body is that outsourcing can, for example, make use of specialist skills, draw on local relationships and increase access to marginalised groups. Additionally, voluntary organisations providing such services can often draw on volunteers and funding sources not accessible to public bodies. In the current financial climate, many smaller community sector organisations and groups are also turning to commissioning as a source of income. While they may already be providing services on an informal basis, they also want to make the transition to take on contracts.

The Threeways Centre, in Halifax, Calderdale, West Yorkshire, is an example of a community sector organisation that successfully became involved in service provision. Threeways is now a thriving centre based in north Halifax, providing a range of activities and services, including training, conference and sport facilities, volunteering support and community projects, such as the 'grow your own' health project. It is managed by local residents and works in partnership with community groups and partner organisations with the aim to empower and enable people to create a brighter future.

The building it is based in is owned by Calderdale Council and was transferred to local community management in 2010 as part of the Council's community assets transfer scheme. Formerly, it was an empty school building with ongoing maintenance costs to the Council; it is now let out to the Threeways charity on a 125-year leasehold arrangement at £1 per year. Funding from trusts and other sources helped to finance feasibility studies and support the early stages. Although Threeways made losses in the first two years, it now provides a range of services for Calderdale district, has built income streams through lettings, sports, conferences and projects and is a key community hub.

As mentioned in Chapter 1, grants from public bodies are being replaced in many cases with tendering as the mechanism for access to funding, placing increased demands on community groups. This shift presents both opportunities and challenges for community groups, which need to carefully consider the advantages and disadvantages of competitive tendering. This shift may also require a change of legal structure and work to prepare the organisation to be 'contract-ready', with new systems of management, monitoring and financial control. This could be, for example, a community organisation running a project to support older people, commissioned by the council's adult social care department. Services could also include those provided by community enterprises, such as gardening for older people provided on a self-paid basis. In terms of influence, taking on contracts from public bodies to run local services may provide opportunities to influence how they are delivered.

However, groups engaged in delivering commissioned services may feel that, rather than having more influence, they now have less. Contracts may tie down the group's activities to delivering a specific set of targets and outputs. In addition, by taking on contracts, some groups have felt that entering competitive markets changes their way of doing things too much and is leading them away from their original aims and values. Criteria for the contract delivery may mean a shift of focus away from supporting traditional beneficiaries, some of whom cannot be catered for within the new contracted service. Through self-help, local groups may already be providing valuable services on an informal basis and decide to stay with that pathway through fear of changing too much. In other cases, community groups have developed their level of organisation and successfully taken on contracts, making organisational changes without reducing their sense of ownership.

Having a say

Central to building stronger communities is the process of people getting involved in decision-making on issues that affect them. *Having a say* could involve service users, community groups, residents and communities of interest. *Having a say* can include a variety of ways in which communities can directly influence local decisions that affect them. *Having a say* is about participating in decision-making structures provided by public bodies. It is different from *organising for change*, which is more about campaigning and mobilising for direct action to influence policy and practice.

At local level, people can sometimes influence decisions about a local *service*, such as the council's waste collection, a local *issue* or problem, such as house break-ins, or a local *resource*, such as the use of an empty council-owned building. Decisions may also address priorities for the area, such as a village plan. Such decisions may consequently be about short-term issues, such as the use of a library building that is having to close soon, or longer term, such as priorities for a neighbourhood plan. The challenge is how to ensure that *having a say* is effective and empowering for the people involved.

In practice, the term *consultation* can have a variety of meanings, often without clarity on the underlying function. Service users, community groups, residents and communities of interest participating in consultation organised by public bodies will need to be aware that consultation could involve a range of possibilities, such as:

➢ gathering factual information on the *needs* of the local community

➢ gathering soft data on the *views* of the local community

> inviting people to contribute *ideas* on how to solve problems and improve services

> inviting people to comment on *proposals* already drawn up

> identifying *priorities* for the local area to inform a community, village or neighbourhood plan.

This range of options for the process of consultation are often muddled, which does not help the consultation to be carried out effectively.

Public services and voluntary organisations that wish to consult service users, community groups, residents and communities of interest have important roles to play in ensuring the engagement methods they use are effective and empowering. There are a variety of ways public services can involve communities and give them opportunities to influence local decisions. Methods often used by local authorities and other public service providers are public meetings, neighbourhood forums, service user focus groups, and surveys, for instance, door to door or online. Participatory budgeting is becoming increasingly popular and the use of social media has created many new opportunities for new forms of consultation. To be effective, such engagement often needs to include some form of outreach work to involve minority groups, as looked at in Chapter 5.

In practice, the experience of many residents is that public meetings and engagement events run by Local Authorities and other public service providers are disappointing:

'It wasn't really a consultation – it had all been decided before hand'.

'I didn't feel confident to speak – very formal, lots of men in suits'.

'We had a good session – but then heard nothing more about it!'

Practitioners can also work with both service providers and communities to help them make the most of opportunities to influence decisions. Boxes 4.6, 4.7 and 4.8 give ideas on how to do this.

Box 4.6 Having more influence at public meetings

Having more influence at a public meeting can be achieved by:

Preparation

- Organising an information-giving session for participants, so they are more aware of the background issues

▶

- Facilitating discussion on issues that may come up
- Ensuring if one person is to be a 'representative' of a group or network, that members of that group or network agree to this.

During the meeting

- Encouraging participants to speak up and be assertive
- Asking for any jargon to be explained
- Keeping clear notes on main decisions made
- If needed, encouraging the group to request time to consider a proposal and consult its own members.

Follow-up

- Circulating notes or minutes from the meeting
- Helping the group to chase up proposals and promises made
- Helping the group to reflect on how the meeting went and learn from what happened.

> 'It was an awful meeting with a lot of upset-ment
> and I felt all fumigated'.
>
> (Community activist, Swansea)

Box 4.7 Increasing community influence

Practical ways in which communities can increase their level of influence on decision makers are:

- Drawing on facts, figures and expert advice
- Being assertive with straight talking about needs and wants
- Consulting stakeholders in order to engage them in the process of change
- Building alliances with key organisations and groups
- Negotiating – have some benefits to offer and a bottom line in mind
- Using social media to build support and organise petitions
- Taking action – a demonstration can have real impact
- Not being side tracked by delays and distractions.

Adapted from Sostenga's Toolkit *Diversity and Social Justice Within Communities*

Box 4.8 describes different types of engagement methods that are increasingly used by community groups, voluntary organisations and public services. They are included here as interesting examples of current practice. Each of these methods can be used to achieve a different outcome, and all four methods can involve large numbers of people, if facilitated carefully. *Open Space* is useful to quickly generate a lot of ideas; *World Café Technique* is a way to explore ideas in more depth; *Promenade* can be used to identify a set of priorities for local action; and *Participatory Budgeting* is a way to involve people in making decisions about a specific public budget.

Box 4.8 Examples of engagement methods

Open Space. This is a method to create new ideas in a series of open discussion groups that run simultaneously. The session usually starts by agreeing on a key question, for example: What are our area's priorities for the next five years? Themes based on the key question are then invited from participants, with small discussion groups being formed for debate. Participants can join or leave the discussion groups at any time. Following these group sessions, feedback at the plenary session is kept to a minimum. The ideas generated can be written up and used to inform the development of new plans and policies (Harrison, 2008).

World Café Technique. The setting is created to resemble a café with small tables around a large room. Each table has a particular theme. After an introduction, participants circulate in groups between tables to explore different issues at each table, and each table has a facilitator who helps make notes on flip charts. As groups move between tables, the facilitator summarises the main points made by earlier groups and through discussion adds further points. This is a useful method to explore ideas in more depth but needs careful facilitation.

Promenade. This is a useful method to involve a large number of people in establishing priorities on local issues. Flip charts are displayed around the walls of a large room. Each chart contains a number of statements about the area, for example, 'household break-ins are the main problem in this area'. These may have been identified earlier from a local survey or World Café event. After an introduction, participants are invited to circulate in pairs around the room, that is, 'promenade', and vote for the key statements on each chart with which they most strongly agree. If they agree with the statement, they add a coloured sticker to the chart. The resulting pattern of stickers can give an indication of the priorities of those present. The session, using the same charts, can be repeated in different venues in a neighbourhood to build up a picture involving a wide range of local groups. Ideally the final resulting patterns on the charts are encapsulated in plastic and displayed in a

▶

◀

central venue, for example, a supermarket, so the participants can see the results. There are many similar versions to this method, and the one described here can be adapted to the particular setting as needed.

Participatory Budgeting. This is a method where people can vote on the use of a public budget. The budget could be a small pot available to fund local community groups, a budget for use to fund public services in the local neighbourhood or a budget for use across the whole city. It can sometimes involve a single event – for example, in Salford a Big Local lottery budget was voted on at an open event to fund local groups. In other cases, it involves public authorities presenting initial ideas at one session, preparing proposals and then facilitating a further open decision-making session. Reservations about the method are that it can be subject to domination by particular groups who 'bus in' supporters or who are more confident in arguing for particular outcomes. Understanding public finances can also be daunting for any participants unless the details are presented carefully in an accessible manner (Sintomer et al., 2008).

Different engagement methods can be used to achieve different aims. Such possibilities are now described with reference to the seven key features of strong communities introduced in Chapter 1. For example:

> *Active.* Is the aim of using the engagement method to recruit more volunteers and group members?

> *Participative.* Is the aim to build understanding of how the council works, so that community representatives can be more effective in contributing to local decisions?

> *Organised.* Is the aim to consult on the needs of local groups, so that organisational support can be provided to help them achieve their aims?

> *Accepting.* Is the aim to build understanding of different cultural traditions between local groups?

> *Resourceful.* Is the aim to stimulate new initiatives and access to additional resources?

> *Connected.* Is the aim to build links and bring different parts of the community together?

> *Fair.* Is the aim to engage with marginalised groups in order to ensure their voices are heard?

So, as well as working with community groups, practitioners can work with public bodies to help them be clearer about the aims of their engagement activities.

Using the Wheel of Participation with communities

The Wheel of Participation can be used with groups to help them look at the range of their current activities. As shown, the six pathways on the Wheel provide different types of opportunities for communities to build their influence and involve people. Practitioners can support community groups and networks to consider, compare and use these different opportunities. A key question for a group to consider is: In order to achieve our aims, are we on the right pathway and do we have the best mix of activities? Such exploration can help groups be a lot clearer about what they are doing and why, ensuring resources and energies are directed most effectively to achieve their long-term aims. A good place to start is with the group's own set of aims, as discussed in Chapter 3. Often groups get involved in one or two pathways without really considering if they are the best ones to choose. Practitioners can work with groups to look at and make use of the Wheel of Participation through *mapping pathways* – using the mapping chart in Box 4.9 to help the group identify the spread of its current activities. A next step would be to help the group to *compare pathways* – facilitating discussion on pros and cons of using different spokes.

Mapping pathways

The Wheel of Participation presented in Box 4.9 can be used by groups to identify the range of activities they are carrying out. The Wheel can be drawn on a flip chart, and each spoke can be looked at in turn to agree on the level of activity, with five levels for groups to choose from. Having identified a level for each of the spokes, the practitioner can facilitate discussion on the resulting pattern. For example, does the pattern match what the group wants to do? Have they got involved in some activities without really considering if they are the most appropriate ones for their set of aims? The author once worked with a community group in Chapeltown, Leeds to help them look at their pattern of activities in relation to their agreed aims. When the group did this, they were shocked to realise that the two sets of activities and aims did not match very well and that they had drifted over the years into new areas of activity without much longer-term planning. Such reviews, through mapping pathways using the Wheel, can help groups be clearer about their future direction and activities.

Box 4.9 Mapping activities on the Wheel of Participation

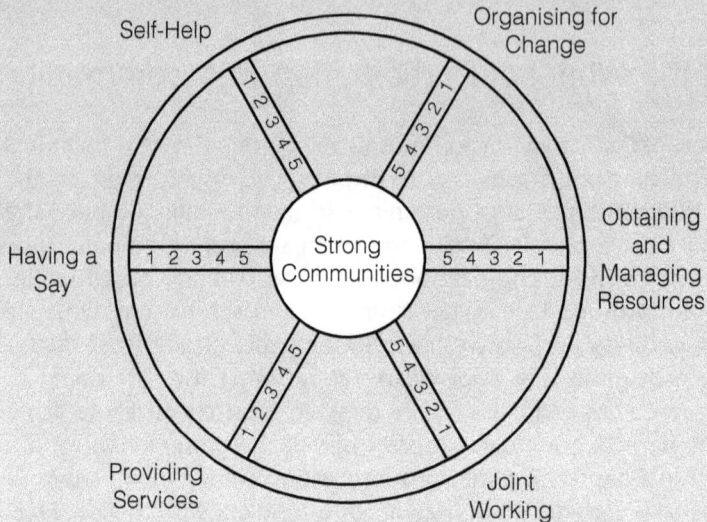

Level one	This type of activity is not carried out in or by our group
Level two	This type of activity is carried out to a minor extent
Level three	This type of activity is carried out to some extent
Level four	This type of activity is carried out to a large extent
Level five	This type of activity is carried out extensively by our group

Comparing pathways

As well as mapping, the Wheel can be used in more depth through a comparison of different pathways. Each pathway provides opportunities as well as limitations to explore with groups. Pros and cons are, for example:

➤ *Self-help activities.* These may focus attention inwards to solve immediate problems and reduce the focus on getting resources from outside sources. However, many groups are involved in self-help activities using mostly their own resources and are providing invaluable social support.

➤ *Organising for change.* This could have great impact, if successful, but may be exhausting.

➤ *Obtaining and managing resources.* Resources can bring new opportunities, but also new responsibilities such as managing a building.

➤ *Joint working.* Joint working may bring funding and new relationships but may place new demands on the group.

➢ *Providing services.* This pathway may increase income, but the activities are now controlled by the terms of the contract.

➢ *Having a say.* Taking this pathway could mean public services offering only tokenistic opportunities for community influence.

Other useful questions to prompt discussion are:

➢ Would certain pathways be more empowering for the group?

➢ Would self-help lead to increased confidence of group members?

➢ Would we lose too much control if we worked jointly with a public body?

➢ Will competitive tendering change our organisation too much?

➢ Which activity will keep us close to our values?

➢ Which activity may take us away from our values?

Such exploration can help groups be a lot clearer about what they are doing and why, ensuring resources and energies are directed most effectively to achieve their long-term aims.

Levels of influence

A key question asked at the start of this chapter was the following: *How can the level of influence over local decisions be strengthened at the grass roots?* Increasing the levels of influence on local decisions at the grass roots is not, for example, merely about being better prepared or presenting a case in a more effective manner. More fundamentally, it is about understanding and using power. In practice, there are a range of positions in relation to power in communities and that inform activities involved, for example, in *having a say.*

Three such positions, called structuralist, pluralist and transformative, were introduced in Chapter 1 (Taylor, 2003). Just to re-cap, a *structuralist* view is where power is seen as being held by a layer of powerful organisations and individuals, who maintain their privileges as a dominant group through control of resources and policy-making. Alternatively, a *pluralist* view sees power as being more spread out and de-centralised and capable of being accessed and shared in a competitive manner (Clegg, 1989). In contrast, a *transformative* view sees power as more fluid in nature, where it can be built and expanded as a resource, rather than just gained or shared.

These three different perspectives on power can be used by practitioners to help community groups, local leaders and active residents think about the positions they hold as beliefs and how these affect their choices for community involvement. Groups may be choosing and using a particular pathway or spoke on the Wheel of Participation because of their strongly held beliefs about power or, alternatively, because they have not really thought about it. The three perspectives can be used to prompt discussion and debate about the group's chosen pathways. For example, does *having a say* imply a pluralist view of power, based on the assumption that there are valid opportunities to influence policy and change local priorities? *Self-help* could be seen as relating to a transformative understanding of power, where participants, through their own initiative and own resources create 'power to' rather than 'power over', in order to achieve their aims. In contrast, *organising for change,* with its campaigning approach, could be seen, in some cases, as being based in a more structuralist view of power – for example, based on the assumption people holding power and associated privileges will not give them up easily.

However, the six pathways on the Wheel of Participation cannot be neatly fitted into three different categories of power. In addition, there will often be cross-overs between pathways, where they are combined in different ways and where priorities change over time. For example, some groups may start with self-help activities but intentionally use it as a way to build local support and then organise a campaign for wider policy changes. Another example of this is the organisation of food banks, where local people collect money to help desperate families; the author has been involved in this in Leeds. With

---

Notes: The design of the Wheel of Participation

The image of a wheel was chosen as a framework for the six pathways for participation and involvement because it presents all the six options as equally valid; all the spokes lead to stronger communities. This gets away from the hierarchy implied, for example, by using the image of a ladder (Arnstein, 1969). The Wheel of Participation is not designed to describe the full range of activities, practices and initiatives that falls under the broader term 'community development', which have been usefully discussed by Twelvetrees (2017). It does not, for example, include the activities involved in forming new groups.

The Wheel does not have a separate pathway for involving volunteers because all of the pathways may involve using volunteers, either in a formal capacity where they are recruited, trained and supported or more informally, where people just help in their street or local centre.

Each pathway has a different *function* and *aim*. For example, *having a say* is about participating in decision-making structures provided by public bodies, whereas *organising for change* is more about communities campaigning and mobilising independently to influence policy and practice. A key point is that the emphasis of the activities and the *intentions* of participants is different in each case. For instance, a group that sets out to *work jointly* with the council to solve a local environmental problem will have different intentions compared to when a group organises their own *self-help* clean-up event, without expecting outside support. As mentioned earlier, pathways may in practice be used in combination and one may be used as a stepping stone to start using another.

such initiatives the question can be asked if raising money for foodbanks is merely helping to maintain inequalities and making the impact of austerity more bearable. However, in practice, campaigns involving raising money for foodbanks have in recent years been based on a more radical aim of eliminating the need for them in the first place.

Vertical and horizontal links

Hopefully, the Wheel of Participation will be a useful tool to help community groups to plan and prioritise future activities. An empowering approach to participation suggests that the emphasis should not always be what could be described as *upwards*, that is, participation between communities and the public sector, but could also, or instead, be *sideways*, in order to build stronger links and networks between local community groups themselves. In this context, it is useful to see community participation as being either *vertical* or *horizontal*, a concept developed by Chanan (1999). This perspective can be applied to the Wheel of Participation, where the emphasis can be on developing either vertical or horizontal relationships. Horizontal participation within the Wheel of Participation could mean, for example:

➢ *Obtaining and managing resources* – local groups joining together with each other to manage a community building.

➢ *Joint working* – two residents' associations agreeing to jointly run an older person's centre.

Vertical participation could mean, for example:

➢ *Having a say* – local residents attend a public meeting to give their views on new proposals on a park presented by the Council.

➢ *Providing services* – a community group is commissioned by the C.C.G. to run a health drop-in centre.

Both vertical and horizontal links will be useful to community groups, depending on their aims. In practice, some groups may struggle to link up very easily with each other because of past tensions and rivalry. Horizontal participation can be a useful initial stage for some groups who then, when more established, choose to engage more with public services. For example, in Bradford in the 1990s, the L.G.B.T. movement, the term they then used, was fragmented and not well-organised; many groups then joined an informal network which eventually elected a representative to sit on the Local Strategic Partnership. Many community groups will, in practice, have a combination of both horizontal and vertical participation, depending on which pathways they are actively involved in.

Being connected is one of the key features of a strong community; some community groups may wish to focus their involvement on building links and relationships with other local groups, rather than directly with the public sector. Some writers see a key aspect of community development as supporting links between groups to build a movement to fight for social justice (Ledwith, 1997).

Summary

Chapter 4 has introduced some key material on strengthening communities:

➤ The Wheel of Participation, with six different approaches to getting communities involved and raising levels of influence at the grass roots.

➤ Different ways to use the Wheel with community groups.

➤ The concept of vertical and horizontal participation.

Key points have been:

➤ The Wheel of Participation could be a useful tool to use with groups to help them make informed choices about their future direction.

➤ The Wheel of Participation is not trying to describe the whole range of community development activity.

➤ Horizontal participation is an important element of strengthening communities.

➤ Practitioners have key roles to play in helping groups to use the Wheel as a planning tool.

The Wheel of Participation demonstrates that there are many different ways in which communities can get involved and have more influence. In these ways, the process of *building involvement* will contribute to creating more *active* and *participative* communities, two of the seven key features used in the definition of 'strong communities'.

Developing your practice

➤ Looking at the Wheel of Participation, which pathways are groups you know involved in?

➤ Which pathways have you been involved in? Why were you involved in these rather than others?

➤ What is your experience of participating in community engagement activities and events run by public service providers? Were these empowering experiences?

➢ How could you build increased horizontal participation between groups?

➢ If you are involving communities in local activities and influencing decision-making, what values will underlie your work as a community practitioner?

Resources

www.lithgow-schmidt.dk/sherry-arnstein/ladder-of-citizen-participation_en.pdf
www.ivar.org.uk
www.corganisers.org.uk
www.tpas.org.uk
www.ctb.ku.edu/en – 'Tools to change the world'
www.jimsimpsonconsultancy.co.uk/wp-content/uploads/2011/05/Empowerment-
    Tools-2-Practicing-participation-methods-and-stages1.pdf

References: Chapter 4

Arnstein, S.R. (1969) *A Ladder of Citizen Participation.* Journal of the American Planning Association, 35 (4).

Cahn, E. (2000) *No More Throw-away People: The Co-Production Imperative.* Washington: Essential Books.

Chanan, G., West, A., Garrett, C. and Humm, J. (1999) *Regeneration and Sustainable Communities.* London: Community Development Foundation.

Clegg, SR. (1989) *Frameworks of Power.* London: Sage.

Harrison, O. (2008) *Open Space Technology: A User's Guide.* 3rd ed. Oakland, CA: Berrett-Koehler.

Hornung, L., Egan, J. and Jochum, V. (2017) *Getting Involved: How People Make a Difference.* London: NCVO.

Kretzmann, J. and McKnight, J. (1993) *Building Communities from the Inside Out.* Illinois: ACTA Publications.

Ledwith, M. (1997) *Community Development: A Critical Approach.* Birmingham: Venture Press.

Putman, R. (2000) *Bowling Alone: The Collapse and Revival of American Community.* New York: Simon and Schuster Paperbacks.

Sintomer, Y., Herzberg, C. and Röcke, A. (2008) *From Porto Alegre to Europe: Potentials and Limitations of Participatory Budgeting.* Erkner, Germany: International Journal of Urban and Regional Research.

Taylor, M. (2003) *Public Policy in the Community.* London: Red Globe Press.

Treasury, H.M. (2005) *Exploring the Role of the Third Sector in Public Service Delivery and Reform.* London: HM Treasury, DTI and Home Office.

Twelvetrees, A. (2017) *Community Development, Social Action and Social Planning.* London: Red Globe Press.

Wales Council for Voluntary Action (2017). Cardiff: WCVA.

5

Building Equality

The previous three chapters explored individual learning, the development of community groups and how communities can get more involved in activities and decision-making. These activities, programmes and initiatives need to be firmly based on a set of values. In this chapter, this issue is explored, looking at how principles of diversity, inclusion and equal opportunities can be applied by practitioners in their work on strengthening communities. *Building equality*, as a short-hand term for this process, is discussed here in its own chapter but, in practice, equality issues need to underlie and inform all aspects of strengthening communities. This agenda is all the more crucial in the current climate where, as described in Chapter 1, tensions have been on the increase. Part One in this chapter explores *building equality* with groups; Part Two looks at the art of developing networks.

Part One: Building equality with groups

Inequality is entrenched in our communities and maintained through a complex combination of factors (Kivisto and Croll, 2012). As a result, some people are not obtaining a fair share of services and resources in their community and, in many cases, they remain marginalised and excluded. Consequently, strengthening communities needs to address essential issues where people are subject to prejudice and discrimination, for example, due to the characteristics protected in law under the Equality Act, 2010.

However, this chapter is not a general introduction to equality and cohesion issues, which have been perceptively discussed by writers such as Gilchrist (2004a), Thompson (2011) and Shaw and Mayo (2016). Instead, the focus is on applying equality issues to the practice of strengthening communities, as explored so far in this book. The term *equality issues* is used to mean the three key elements of *diversity, inclusion* and *equal opportunities*. These are now discussed in turn, with practical examples of supporting and challenging groups.

Equality issues

Valuing *diversity* means recognising differences, where we see people as individuals and respond to them positively in an individual manner (Stones, 2018). In contrast, discrimination can be seen as a process of basing relationships on stereotypes and attributing negative characteristics to certain groups of people (Thompson, 2011). Discrimination can be defined as differential treatment of people assigned to particular social categories (Bagilhole, 2009). However, valuing diversity is not just about 'tolerating' difference but seeing differences in communities as bringing positive benefits. It is not about seeing some groups on the margins as a problem but appreciating the rich spread of differences that exist across all communities. The promotion of diversity has recently focused more on building on such positive approaches, rather than just trying to tackle the negatives (Thompson, 2011). However, it is also important that the positive approach to promoting diversity is not at the cost of recognising and tackling discrimination.

Applying the principle of *inclusion* means using policies and practices in which groups or individuals with different backgrounds and identities are treated fairly and not excluded. Treating people fairly does not mean treating everyone in the same way; we need to recognise difference and respond appropriately (Wetherly, 2017). Promoting and valuing diversity in communities needs to be complemented with inclusion policies and practices in order to avoid creating communities as a series of cultural 'silos'. For instance, the Cantle report, written following civil unrest in Bradford, discussed how different cultural groups could exist in the urban areas with little real contact and connections (Cantle, 2001). The report argued that a multi-cultural approach to funding community groups based on cultural identity had, in effect, reinforced the separation between different groups. The author worked in Bradford at that time and saw this pattern first-hand. It needs to be appreciated that initiatives based on a cohesion approach are not easy to implement and should not be a substitute for addressing the underlying issues of the unfair allocation of public resources (Gilchrist, 2004a).

The concept of *equal opportunities* is a valid starting point in addressing equalities issues. It involves, in this context, the provision of equal access to resources and support for strengthening communities; for example, ensuring that a training course for community groups is equally open to men and women. A second, very useful, concept is *equality of condition*, meaning not only equality of access but also recognising the varying conditions of life for different social groups (Bagilhole, 2009). In other words, equal access may not solve the problem, as people are starting from different points. The conditions where they start from are not equal – it is not a level playing field. Given such inequalities, practitioners need to be pro-active in tackling underlying barriers to participation.

Box 5.1 Examples of inclusion

In Beeston, Leeds, residents organised a hiking weekend to climb Ben Nevis. It came out of several day trips to Wales, building on community involvement work across a diverse area, covering the LS10 and LS11 areas of Leeds. The weekend was self-financing, with a borrowed mini-bus, and involved people from a wide range of faiths and identities, including a homeless man. The trip helped to build understanding and friendships between different cultural groups, not only through walking together but also through shared meals. The shared task of organising the trip was a key part of the collaboration and cooperation.

In Pendle, East Lancashire, community relations were improved between the local white and south Asian communities through a project with US artist, Suzanne Lacey and an artists' collective, In-Situ. The project began in 2016 and lasted 18 months. Suzanne worked closely with Pendle residents in a series of community meetings and singing sessions, exploring the history of the area and different vocal traditions that exist there. She brought people from all walks of life together to share food, culture and experiences, culminating in a mass community celebration at the former Smith and Nephew Mill in Brierfield. The resulting new artwork, *Shapes of Water, Sounds of Hope*, was produced over three days at the mill between 29 September and 1 October. Residents were invited to take part by observing performances, participating in singing sessions and coming to a large banquet for 500 people, which took place on the ground floor of the mill. They were able to share their stories and experiences of the mill and living in Pendle in the largest event of its kind the area has ever seen. The project, which ran for over 18 months, was commissioned by Super Slow Way as part of the Creative People and Places programme.

In Hampshire, a radio station is using social media to involve older people and break down social isolation. The radio station is designing programmes especially for care homes in the neighbouring area, working with a local musician. The radio shows are based on a sing-along session, with individual songs dedicated to individuals in different care homes. During the show, a Facebook thread is used to involve listeners in online conversation.

Supporting groups on equality issues

Practitioners can work with community groups in different ways to explore issues of diversity, inclusion and equal opportunities. This can include acting as facilitators as described in Box 5.2 or helping groups to broaden the diversity of contacts and relationships, as described in Box 5.3. The Five Steps method described in Box 5.4 can be used by community groups to look at how they could increase involvement of other groups of people with different backgrounds. However, these are only examples of a range of methods; see Resources at the end of this chapter for toolkits.

Some groups may take the view they just want to get on with doing things rather than spend time 'discussing equality'. Practitioners can act in a challenging role here to prompt a better understanding and how in practice 'getting things done' will often involve issues of equality, diversity and inclusion.

Box 5.2 Starting out on equality issues

Practitioners can help community groups to consider the wider issues of equal opportunities and diversity, by, for example:

- Inviting groups to look at the backgrounds of their members and how much these reflect the diversity of the local community

- Helping groups to create a 'statement of intent' on equality issues – that is, a tailor-made statement on values and practices

- Working with groups to create an action plan on equality issues – where, in the light of awareness raising and a statement of intention, the group draws up plans to address equality issues and tackle barriers to wider participation in the group's activities.

Such support is only a beginning, but it is a useful way to work with and challenge groups on equality issues.

Box 5.3 Supporting a community group with diversity issues

Groups can be supported to broaden the diversity of contacts and relationships with other groups by using a simple visual exercise:

- Draw a circle in the middle of a flip chart and write on it the name of the group.

- Invite group members to call out the names of other groups in their neighbourhood, city or network who they perceive as marginalised or under-represented.

- Write the name of each marginalised group on a sticky note and place the note on the flip chart near or far from the middle circle.

- In placing each sticky note around the middle circle, ask the group how near or far it should be placed, moving the note around as needed. In each case, the distance from the middle circle to the note needs to reflect the closeness of the link. A short line would indicate a close working relationship, such as a jointly run project, whereas a long line would indicate a low level of links or contact.

◀

- After a range of groups are shown located around the middle circle, ask the group to choose those with which they especially want to have more contact in the coming year.

- An action plan can be drawn up on how this increased contact can be made.

This is a simple planning method that can help groups to reflect on their web of relationships and begin to address gaps and barriers. A further step is to help the group discuss, in the light of the activity, how marginalised they perceive themselves as.

Box 5.4 The Five Steps method

The Five Steps method can be used by community groups to look at how to increase the involvement of people with different backgrounds.

Step One – The Reality. Start by identifying a particular group of people who live in the area but that your centre or organisation currently has no contact with, such as Eastern Europeans or white working-class men. Possible questions to ask are:

- How welcoming is our building to people with different backgrounds?

- What images do we use in our publicity for activities?

- What assumptions do our members make about people from this background?

Step Two – The Ideal. Think of how it could be in future:

- What would we like to see happen?

- What would a better picture look like?

Step Three – The Benefits. By involving more people from this background:

- What could be the benefits?

- How could involving more people make us stronger as a group?

Step Four – The Barriers. There might be blocks and barriers that prevent the changes from happening:

- What barriers might get in the way?

- Are these barriers personal, such as attitudes?

- Are these barriers organisational, such as the layout of the building we use?

Step Five – The Ways Forward. These are practical steps that can be taken:

- How can each of the barriers be tackled?

- How can we move towards our ideal?

- What are the first actions we need to take?

Addressing equality issues in community capacity building

In order to address equality issues in community capacity building (CCB) activities, a framework can be used consisting of three headings, adapted from one described by Gilchrist (2007): practical, psychological and political.

Practical

The 'practical' approach is partly about identifying and tackling barriers to participation by different groups and communities in CCB activities and programmes. Some people may be reluctant to participate in community activities as they may feel low on confidence or alienated in some way. Others may want to become involved but face barriers that deter them, such as buildings that are inaccessible, venues that are hard to get to, seating layout that seems very formal or training presentations that are full of jargon. Different communities may experience different types of barriers. For instance, some minority groups may not be in touch with mainstream networks and communication channels and thus miss out on invitations to training events. Lack of transport in rural or isolated areas can be a barrier for people to get to meetings and events.

So, in planning CCB activities with groups, practitioners could facilitate discussion on a number of questions: What minority groups are there in the area? Will the event that is being planned appeal to different communities? Is the event being held in a venue, for example, a pub, that will exclude some people?

Other key issues include access – Will people find it difficult to get to the venue? Is the venue accessible for people using wheelchairs? What types of events will create opportunities for people of different backgrounds to be involved? Will participants need to read and write well in English in order to participate? Is access to CCB activities and programmes dependent on owning a computer or smart phone?

> 'We organised a community festival: – it was a great way to involve many different people in the area, as there were many different ways to get involved and learn new skills.'

> (Ward Councillor, West Midlands)

> ## Box 5.5 The content of community capacity building
>
> The values of equal opportunities, inclusion and diversity also need to apply to the *content* of community capacity building. Issues to consider are:
>
> - Do the training materials reflect a diversity of cultural perspectives?
> - Do examples used in training reflect the experiences of different groups?
> - Do images of people used in presentations show a diversity of identities?
> - In feedback and discussions, are different cultural perspectives welcomed?
> - Are existing power relationships in the community ever challenged?
> - Do men always take leading roles in discussions?
> - Are transgender people welcomed?
> - Does the evaluation of the training consider diversity and equality issues?
> - Overall, is CCB increasing understanding and acceptance between different groups in the community?

Psychological

As indicated above, discrimination can be seen as a process of attributing stereotypes and negative characteristics to certain groups of people (Thompson, 2011), and there will be a psychological side to such discrimination that needs unearthing and addressing. Sometimes biases and prejudice will be conscious and deliberate, whilst in other cases people may be unaware of their own attitudes. So, compared to practical barriers that are *visible*, there are also many powerful *invisible barriers,* such as attitudes that put people off getting involved:

'Everywhere I go, I am seen as a problem.'

(Gypsy Traveller, North Yorkshire)

In some cases, members of faith-based groups fear they will experience prejudice from members of other community groups. Misinformation can feed stereotypes, which in turn become normalised into 'common knowledge' and 'how things are'! Shifts are needed so that people recognise how we are all different in some way and that differences can enrich our communities. In other words, diversity is more than just tolerating difference; it also is about valuing, affirming and celebrating difference. This needs to be through honest, personal reflection and change and not just adherence to a new set of jargon or using politically correct phrases.

Practitioners can act as facilitators with groups to explore these issues, both challenging and supporting people to look at their attitudes and assumptions. Methods for this, as discussed in Chapter 2, could include, for example, awareness-raising sessions, workshops, visits and arts projects. This is demanding work and requires that the practitioner be comfortable with their own views and feelings on equality issues. Also, some group members might be resistant to change, especially in cases where they may lose certain privileges or advantages. Such changes in attitudes and behaviour usually take place in stages over time and require leadership and perseverance (Gilchrist, 2007).

Political

The term 'political' is used here with a small 'p', referring to the distribution of power and resources in communities. While addressing the psychological side of discrimination is important, it is not enough without considering the wider context. Equally, barriers to participation are a reflection of deeper processes of discrimination and imbalances in access to power at community level (Taylor, 2003). It is essential that divisions in communities are not reinforced by community capacity building initiatives. Practitioners need to consider questions such as the following: Which individuals are taking up development opportunities, as discussed in Chapter 2? Which groups are obtaining support, as described in Chapter 3? Which groups and individuals are involved in increased levels of influence, as explored in Chapter 4? It is worth thinking about who is already actively involved in the community and who is missing; there may be some people or groups that are not involved at all but who, with appropriate support, would be keen to participate. Urban bias also needs to be considered, where rural or semi-rural areas may be excluded from CCB initiatives (Bell and Oakley, 2015). Some community groups are called 'hard to reach' but:

'We are not hard to reach – the Council is!'

(Disability leader, Leeds)

In looking at the bigger picture, useful points to consider are: Is CCB equally available to different groups? Is 'strengthening communities' mainly about involving groups on the margins? Will CCB largely benefit already well-established, more confident groups? Are opportunities for learning and organisational support being presented in ways that alienate some groups? Are local learning opportunities open to everyone in the community? More fundamentally, is CCB provision being 'colour-blind' to diversity and, by treating everyone the same, is it in practice excluding some people? Is support, in effect, favouring those with stronger voices? By participating, will some groups feel empowered but others be left out?

Experience from poorer countries shows that CCB is a resource that can either be used to support a wide range of groups or, in effect, be controlled by a dominant minority (Eade and Williams, 1995). For example, in one case a CCB programme led to the strengthening of a group of men ruling the village, where women were discriminated against. Also, in order to be able to participate in support activities, some groups may need what can be called a *safe space* – being in an environment closed to people of other identities. An Asian women's group, for example, may wish to have a women-only training session. Increasingly, transgender issues are being debated in this context. These are controversial and complex issues that practitioners now need to consider in their work.

'Outreach' work is one way to identify and involve groups that exist on the margins and are being excluded in different ways. Such work is more pro-active than just focusing on reducing barriers to participation. Some basic practice points in outreach work are:

➤ Make use of local networks, both formal and informal, to make contacts; one local group will often know others.

➤ Contact voluntary organisations whose members already work with marginalised groups.

➤ Ask to visit the group – groups will often appreciate such a request.

➤ Ask the group members what they see as the best way to involve them in future and what they see as barriers to their participation.

Some groups may not have leaders in any formal roles, such as a chairperson; they may not have committees or annual general meetings but still be providing valuable social support and engaging in campaigning work in their own communities (Bolton, 2017). In organising a programme of support in inner-city Bradford, the author, working with other community workers, became involved in outreach work to identify and build up contacts with community groups that were not already on the existing groups' database. They got to know the members of a tiny, back-street Hindu temple who, once contacted, were very interested in participating in local networks and meeting other groups in the area.

Box 5.6 An example of outreach: The Laco project in Bradford

Laco is a project established by the Thornbury Centre in Bradford which has been involved in innovative community development work with Eastern European communities, with a particular focus on Roma communities. From 2004, Roma people began settling in Bradford from various parts of Eastern Europe. Outreach and engagement work has been based in different parts of Bradford and funded by a range of organisations, including Bradford's Greenmoor Big Local programme. Laco means 'good' in Slovakian; the approach taken has been to work with and through the use of what are seen by the community as 'trusted places', in this case the Thornbury Centre, local schools and children's centres.

Key to success in this work was employing Roma, as well as white Polish or Slovakian residents, as community workers, with on-the-job training. Working in partnership with other organisations to provide welfare benefits advice sessions, the project also got Roma residents involved through going door to door and social events. The activities Laco provided were family based, with an emphasis on building trust. The project found that each Roma community is different, depending on their country of origin. The Roma communities were spread out across the city, and different approaches were needed. Advice sessions and assistance in getting paid work worked well in all areas. Once these basic relationships were established, Laco focused on improving health and well-being, and also helping people to recognise their rights and responsibilities as members of their new Bradford community.

Outreach work could also include finding out about specific needs of marginalised groups in terms of community capacity building. In Chapter 3, 'community strengths profiles' were described, based on geographical areas such as a ward, neighbourhood or town. However, some communities of interest may not be based in a locality, so consequently an assessment of their CCB needs may have to be more targeted on particular networks of groups.

Such outreach work also raises wider political issues: Is such outreach work with communities of interest in effect ignoring the needs of geographically based poor communities? For example, some tenants' associations in areas of social housing represent and involve people on low incomes, though they may not be marginalised in the conventional sense of the term. In other words, practitioners need to consider *class* issues, as well as the needs of particular communities of interest. Work to strengthen communities needs to build links and relationships between communities of interest and other communities, rather than further divide people. In this context, it has been argued that building alliances within and between communities needs to be informed by both an appreciation of diversity issues and an understanding of social class (Shaw and Mayo, 2016).

Different practical initiatives to tackle barriers and negative attitudes also need to be reinforced by policies on equality issues being in place, both in community groups and in larger public and voluntary sector organisations. For example, community groups can devise and adopt policies on equal opportunities, diversity and inclusion. This needs to be done in ways that really mean something to participants and is not just a tick-the-box exercise. When planning new projects, groups can integrate equality goals into their sets of aims and objectives, as discussed in Chapter 3. Additionally, practitioners can support community groups to use existing frameworks, such as the Scottish National Standards for Community Engagement as described in Box 5.7, to inform both practice and policy development.

Further discussion on policies to support CCB is in Chapter 6. The role of networks and networking as a part of *building equality* is now explored.

Box 5.7 The Scottish National Standards for Community Engagement

The National Standards for Community Engagement have been developed in Scotland and are a very useful framework for community groups and public sector organisations. Each of the standards includes a short headline statement and a set of indicators to show progress towards meeting each standard. For example, the heading for the standard called *Inclusion* is:

> We will identify and involve the people and organisations that are affected by the focus of the engagement.

Their guidelines then ask: How will we know we have met this Standard?

- The people and groups who are affected by the focus of the engagement are involved at the earliest opportunity.

- Measures are taken to involve groups with protected characteristics and people who are excluded from participating due to disadvantage relating to social or economic factors.

- Participants in the community engagement process commit to continued two-way communication with the people they work with or represent.

- A wide range of opinions, including minority and opposing views, are valued in the engagement process.

Protected characteristics refers to groups defined in the Equality Act, 2010.

Part Two: Working with networks

Networks, both informal and formal, are important for strengthening communities because they can attract and involve marginalised groups and can be a useful channel for learning and change. Consequently, helping to build networks of both marginalised and mainstream groups is especially important in *building equality*. Part Two now explores ways to do this.

There is a difference between social networks, consisting of personal contacts belonging to individuals that provide them with support and resources (Halpern, 2005; Hobsbawn, 2018), and networks of community groups, where such groups have contacts and links with other groups. In practice, there is extensive overlap between these two different types of networks. Research on the role of *social networks* in addressing poverty has identified a range of benefits and uses of such networks, such as providing mutual support, improving local services, raising aspirations and acting as the basis for collective action and campaigning (Afridi, 2011). Many networks are now based online, where social media can act as a channel for community action. However, there is a lack of research on the use of social media by grass roots community groups (Harris and McCabe, 2017).

Networks of groups may be very informal, based, for example, on a particular neighbourhood or village, and can be developed into more formal structures, such as federations and coalitions. Networks are usually not hierarchical in structure and can be used for effective collaboration and consultation.

Networks of people with a particular concern or experience, such as being a carer or having a disability, have also been widely used by public sector organisations and partnerships as the basis for community representation to influence decisions on local services. In many areas, voluntary sector 'assemblies' act as networks to bring together different identity groups to elect or select representatives for decision-making partnerships.

While *networks* are structures, either formally or informally organised, *networking* is a process, though the two terms are often mixed up. Too often the term 'networking' is used without any real clarity as to its purpose, as if it is a valid end in its own right:

'We used to meet up for a coffee and a chat – now it's called networking!'

(Community worker, Leeds)

Research has shown that networking can carry out a range of functions, such as exchanging information and views, joint working to gain support and influence policy, and coordinating work in an area. Other useful functions are the exchange of skills and knowledge, sharing support and building confidence, developing a sense of common purpose, and forming the basis for community representation (Gilchrist, 2004b). Given this range of functions, networking can be a useful tool for strengthening communities, in particular to build *active, participative* and *connected* communities. It has also been argued that effective networking can increase people's options and opportunities (D'Souza, 2011).

Practitioners can support community groups and, in particular, marginalised communities of interest, through helping them develop and make good use of networks and networking. This could be by looking at the range of roles networks can carry out, as described in Box 5.8. Box 5.9 helps groups that are using social media to be clearer about methods and messages.

Box 5.8 Reviewing networks

Groups can review how much they are benefiting from being involved in different networks by looking at the range of roles networks can carry out and deciding to what extent each role is useful for them. To do this, ask the group to choose a network they are in, then facilitate discussion on each of the various roles carried out by that network. A range of possible roles (Gilchrist, 2004b) are:

- Exchanging information and views
- Joint working to gain support and influence policy
- Coordinating work in our area
- Exchanging skills and knowledge
- Sharing support and building confidence
- Developing a sense of common purpose
- Forming the basis for community representation.

Then for each role in turn, ask: By being in this network, how useful is that role for our group? The scoring can be 1–5, where 1 is low and 5 is high. This activity can lead to discussion on how much the group is benefiting and whether changes are needed. Other useful questions are:

- What barriers prevent us from benefiting more?
- What actions are needed to address these barriers?

Box 5.9 Checklist on using social media

Social media can be a powerful tool for networking between community groups (Harris and McCabe, 2017). However, there is a need for groups to be clear about methods and messages at an early stage. Practitioners can help groups to review their use by asking:

- Why do you want to use social media? What are your aims?
- What messages do you want to communicate?
- Who are you trying to reach? Which method will reach them most effectively?
- Who is speaking on behalf of your group?
- Can you keep your personal and work-related sites separate?
- Is your information correct?
- Have you checked your permissions on the site?
- Do you have the time to keep the site updated, or do you need someone to help you do this?

To build local links, social media needs to be about communicating and exchanging, not just broadcasting.

Concluding points

This chapter has briefly explored how the principles of equal opportunities, diversity and inclusion can inform practitioners' work on strengthening communities. Key questions arising from the discussion of equalities issues are: Who is being empowered? Who is not involved? Who is dominating the process? How can we help to build networks that involve minorities? The values of equal opportunities, inclusion and diversity need to inform and underlie work with communities. As a practitioner, you have choices to make about your approach to community empowerment and how you can base it on the values explored in this chapter.

Summary

Chapter 5 has covered some key material on *building equality*. It looked at:

➢ Barriers to involvement in community capacity building (CCB)

➢ Ways to reach out to marginalised groups

➢ Networks and networking as ways to involve minorities and build links between different groups.

Key points have been that:

> The values of equal opportunity, diversity and inclusion need to inform the work of strengthening communities.

> Without careful planning, CCB programmes can support the already dominant position of certain groups.

> Equalities values can be explored in CCB by considering practical, personal and political issues.

Building equality suggests community empowerment needs to be underpinned by a strong values base. It emphasises the importance of working with and supporting excluded and marginalised groups and actively facilitating links between groups of different identities and backgrounds.

Developing your practice

Building equality needs to inform and inspire how practitioners work with:

> *Individuals* – in developing new practices and especially challenging prejudice and discrimination.

> *Groups* – in contacting and supporting marginalised groups to have access to mainstream opportunities for CCB.

> *Communities* – in helping build bridges between different cultural groups.

Actively challenging discrimination in groups is a key part of *building equality*. For example, when you hear a discriminatory remark, the first thing is not to reinforce it by ignoring it. Also, be prepared to respond to prejudice and misinformation. More fundamentally, this chapter has promoted certain values which need to inform the work of practitioners. These values cannot just be adopted as a practical method but need to be based on your own exploration of your practice and beliefs.

Start with yourself – you could talk through these questions with a colleague or friend:

> In your life, when have you ever felt left out or marginalised? How did this experience affect your confidence?

> How can you broaden your own experiences of different cultures and identities?

> What support can you obtain to help to strengthen your awareness of these issues?

Consider your priorities about who the work is for – you could talk these questions through with your employer or the chairperson of your group:

➢ Are you working with groups with whom you feel 'at home', that are the same cultural background as you? Are you, in effect, ignoring requests for support from other groups?

➢ If you are a Hindu, do you only work with Hindu groups? If you are a Christian, do you mainly work with Christian groups?

➢ Do you ever do any outreach to 'seldom heard' groups?

➢ How will the values of equal opportunities and diversity inform your future priorities as a practitioner?

Don't work alone – consider teaming up with someone of a different cultural background from yourself, working together and learning from each other.

Box 5.10 How not to organise community capacity building

If you really want to mess things up, here are a few helpful tips:

• Arrange the training event to clash with a major religious holiday.

• Only advertise it on the internet and as late as possible.

• Include a lot of jargon in the publicity.

• Use a venue that is hard to find and without wheelchair access.

• Start with a long PowerPoint presentation that no one understands.

• Do not listen to different views.

• Only listen to those who shout loudest or agree with you.

• Assume everyone can read in English and has access to a computer.

Resources

www.communityplanningtoolkit.org/sites/default/files/Engagement.pdf
www.scdc.org.uk/what/national-standards/10-national-standards/
www.scdc.org.uk/what/voice
www.PeopleandParticipation.net
www.communityplaces.info

www.networkedcity.london/networks/index
www.networkedcity.london/networks/ecosys
www.superslowway.org.uk/projects/shapes-of-water-sounds-of-hope/

References: Chapter 5

Afridi, A. (2011) *Social Networks: Their Role in Addressing Poverty*. York: Joseph
     Rowntree Foundation.

Bagilhole, B. (2009) *Understanding Equal Opportunities and Diversity*. Bristol: Policy
     Press.

Bell, D. and Oakley, K. (2015) *Cultural Policy*. New York: Routledge.

Bolton, M. (2017) *How to Resist: Turn Protest to Power*. London: Bloomsbury.

Cantle, T. (2001) *Community Cohesion: A Report of the Independent Review Team*.
     London: Home Office.

D'Souza, S. (2011) *Brilliant Networking*. Harlow: Prentice Hall.

Eade, D. and Williams, S. (1995) *The Oxfam Handbook of Development and Relief*.
     Oxford: Oxfam.

Gilchrist, A. (2004a) *Community Cohesion and Community Development*. London: The
     Community Development Foundation.

Gilchrist, A. (2004b) *The Well-Connected Community: A Networking Approach to
     Community Development*. Bristol: Policy Press.

Gilchrist, A. (2006b) *Community Development and Networking*. London: The
     Community Development Foundation.

Gilchrist, A. (2007) *Equalities and Communities*. London: The Community
     Development Foundation.

Halpern, D. (2005) *Social Capital*. Cambridge: Polity Press.

Harris, K. and McCabe, A. (2017) *A Community Action and Social Media: Trouble in
     Utopia? Briefing Paper 140*. Birmingham: Third Sector Research Centre.

Hobsbawn, M.J. (2018) *Fully Connected*. London: Bloomsbury Business.

Kivisto, P. and Croll, P. (2012) *Race and Ethnicity*. Oxon: Routledge.

Shaw, M. and Mayo, M. (2016) *Class, Inequality and Community Development*.
     Bristol: Policy Press.

Stones, J. (2018) *Cultural Theory and Popular Culture*. New York: Routledge.

Taylor, M. (2003) *Public Policy in the Community*. London: Red Globe Press.

Thompson, N. (2011) *Promoting Equality*. London: Red Globe Press.

6

A Partnership Approach

The four themes of *Building Organisation, Building People, Building Involvement* and *Building Equality* create a useful framework for the policy and practical work involved in strengthening communities. As discussed, these four themes are not silos but are best used in combination, with *building equality* informing the practice and activities in the other three thematic areas.

The emphasis in this book has been on working at and with the grass roots, using a bottom-up approach and valuing the assets and strengths that individuals and groups already have. It has focused on the work of individual practitioners, based in a variety of settings. However, strengthening communities also needs the active support of the public sector in order to be effective; in this final chapter, what this support could mean is explored, based on a partnership approach. Consequently, the focus of this chapter is on what large organisations can do, rather than on individual practitioners, in order to contribute to strengthening communities. It looks at the roles that can be played by public sector organisations, in particular, local authorities. It also briefly discusses how private sector organisations interested in corporate social responsibility can get involved.

A partnership approach generally also means the community and voluntary sectors, as defined in Chapter 1, work jointly with other sectors in order to more effectively organise and coordinate efforts to build stronger communities. Many voluntary sector organisations are already providing valuable services of various kinds to support voluntary and community groups in their areas. For example, in Wales, these are county-based organisations and called County Voluntary Councils. There are similar structures in other parts of the UK, but the coverage is not so comprehensive as in Wales. In the current climate, such infrastructure organisations have often been facing reduced budgets from funders.

A wide range of public service providers, such as local authorities, health services, schools, housing associations, universities and police forces are already involved in *community engagement*, using a variety of methods and approaches. However, this range of engagement, as commonly practiced, often is not enough to effectively build stronger communities. It needs to be extended to also actively and directly support community capacity building, based on the underlying principles of equality and empowerment.

The role of public services

A key question is: *Why should public service providers be interested in building strong communities?* Public services can benefit from stronger communities in a variety of ways, at both operational and strategic levels. At operational level, active local community groups and networks can fulfil many useful roles, such as contributing volunteers and practical help and bringing additional resources to the delivery of services, for example, in adult social care or leisure activities. Community groups may also have access to funding, such as the Lottery and other trusts, not available to Councils. Groups and user networks can also be a source of people to act as representatives on public bodies, bringing local knowledge and information to inform the design of services. Additionally, community groups can also act as partners to provide services, as discussed in Chapter 4 (Cahn, 2001). While still small in scale, increasingly community groups are entering the market for tendering in order to deliver specialist services.

For many public sector organisations, building strong communities will match their own long-term strategic aims. There is a range of ways such outcomes can be measured (Chanan, 2002). Increasingly, policy-makers are valuing the role of social capital, where community groups and activities provide a bedrock of social support and informal activities that complements the provision of formal services (Parsfield et al., 2015). In addition, a number of studies have estimated substantial health savings arising from greater community involvement (Chanan and Fisher, 2017). In Preston, for instance, the 'Preston Model' of local procurement and commissioning has demonstrated the benefits arising from building enterprise capacity at local level.

Practitioners can work with public services to develop practices and policies that strengthen and empower communities at the grass roots.

For public sector organisations, support for strengthening communities can be described as containing at least three main options. These are:

➤ supporting and implementing community capacity building (CCB)

➤ producing a joint strategy on strengthening communities

➤ organising agency capacity building.

These three approaches are now explored in turn.

Supporting community capacity building

Public service providers can support community capacity building activities and initiatives in a variety of ways (Skinner, 1997). The four themes used earlier in this book for strengthening communities are useful categories, as shown in Box 6.1. Obviously, resourcing such initiatives in the current climate is a challenge. However, despite this, some local authorities and other public service organisations continue to fund such additional activities as a priority. Actually, some initiatives do not involve additional expenditure; for example, the University of Bradford opened up its in-house staff training programme to members of community groups. The scheme was inexpensive to run and very successful, enhancing the learning environment for all participants.

Box 6.1 provides a list of possibilities; the list can be used by public services to draw up an action plan, based on discussion with representatives from the voluntary and community sectors. However, in contrast to activities and practices described in the previous chapters, these suggested actions would be organised by public sector organisations, rather than by individual practitioners. They mainly require action and resources allocated at management levels. Community groups and practitioners may well have constructive roles to play in facilitating and advising on such initiatives.

Box 6.1 Supporting community capacity building

Activities that public sector organisations can carry out:

Building people

- Set up a small grants programme aiming to specifically build the skills of members of community groups.

- Open up in-house training with free places for members of community groups.

- Support a network of community hubs that act as learning centres for local groups. Recent research indicates the potential for libraries to take on these roles (Grimsey, 2018).

- Support learning online for members of community groups by providing equipment and technical backup.

- Provide mentoring in leadership and management for community leaders.

Building organisations

- Support a network of community hubs that act as resource centres for local groups.

- Fund voluntary sector infrastructure organisations to be able to effectively provide advice and support to groups.

- Set up a small grants programme with criteria to specifically build the strengths of community groups.

▶

◀

- Make space available in local public buildings for groups to meet, with access to computers and printing equipment.

- Ensure staff are available, with appropriate training, job descriptions and skills, to help community groups develop their organisations, projects and activities.

Building involvement

- Support self-help initiatives, with advice, information and provision of facilities.

- Employ staff experienced in community development work to support local initiatives.

- Develop a policy on asset transfer, avoiding the transfer of 'white elephants'.

- Support local groups who wish to engage in meaningful co-production.

- Support local groups who wish to take on the asset transfer of a public building for community use.

- Ensure community engagement is effective, meaningful and based on standards of good practice.

- Help groups to use the Wheel of Participation in planning future activities.

- Support volunteering programmes based on local initiatives, such as Trafford Council's 'Be Bold' programme.

Building equality

- Ensure relationships are built with seldom-heard and 'hard to reach' groups, in order to avoid them being excluded from CCB programmes.

- Maintain an up-to-date, comprehensive directory of community and voluntary groups or fund a voluntary sector infrastructure organisation properly to do this.

- Fund initiatives that involve outreach to excluded groups.

- Support networks and networking activities that specifically engage with excluded groups.

- Adopt a policy on CCB that explicitly supports equal opportunities and the promotion of inclusion and diversity.

Organising such initiatives will need liaison with voluntary sector infrastructure organisations who carry out essential support for front-line community groups. In 2015, there were around 800 active voluntary sector infrastructure organisations in England and Wales. The majority of them worked on a local basis, including more than 350 Councils for Voluntary Service (CVSs), over 200 Volunteer Centres, Rural Community Councils and specialist local bodies (NCVO, 2015). Given the current climate, these figures may well have gone down since 2015. Research by the National Council for Voluntary Organisations indicates that local infrastructure organisations carry out a range of roles, including acting as umbrella bodies; providing services to frontline groups; providing buildings, facilities and human resources support; and channelling grants to local organisations (NCVO, 2015). In some cases, this type of support is being provided by more locally based community organisations, such as development trusts and large community centres. Wherever it is based, a key concern is that such support addresses the needs of smaller-scale groups from the community sector, as well as those of larger voluntary organisations.

The private sector also has great potential in supporting community capacity building. There are a range of ways that private sector organisations can contribute to strengthening communities, such as by providing free or subsidised technical support, depending on the company's specialities. Such support could include planning advice, human resources and accountancy services or architectural and legal advice. Companies can contribute to grants programmes by donating directly or through a community foundation. A useful role can also be to provide community leaders with business mentors; usually the mentors also gain a lot from the sessions. Many companies organise staff teams as volunteers to support community groups, where staff also benefit from team building and enhanced communication skills.

Corporate social responsibility can be often carried out as a form of enlightened self-interest (Johnson et al., 2008). Such initiatives can make good business sense for companies by building an enhanced reputation, helping to recruit and retain staff, as well as providing opportunities for professional development. So, rather than such activities just being seen as a one-way transfer of support, companies can learn from the experience of working with community groups and local leaders in such a way as to enhance the capacity of staff teams and managers (Johnson et al., 2008).

Developing a joint strategy

The support of community capacity building (CCB) ideally needs to be part of a jointly produced strategy on strengthening communities (Skinner, 2006). A CCB strategy could be developed between a range of stakeholders, with the effective involvement of the community and voluntary sectors. Such a 'partnership' should involve representatives at senior level, for example, from the police, public health, schools, higher and further education, the local authority and business forums. A strategy on CCB ideally would contain the following elements:

Aims: The strategy will need a clear statement on aims and outcomes and a commitment to promoting equal opportunities, supporting diversity and addressing inclusion.

Needs: Ideally, devising the strategy would involve producing an overview of *CCB* needs in the city or district, taking into account existing strengths and abilities. Chapter 2 of this book describes one way to do this through carrying out community strengths profiles. These can be carried out in areas of greatest need first and a picture of the whole city or district built up over time. In parallel, strengths profiles would be useful to address the needs and strengths of particular communities of interest. Over time, this profiling can involve a rolling programme across the district of identifying both the needs and the strengths of different communities. However, creating this picture will require outreach work and relationship building to ensure communities feel they have some real part to play in the process.

Resources: These assessments of needs can be examined in the light of an audit of resources available for CCB activities at district or local level. Such an assessment can include a description of staff and any budgetary resources currently being specifically committed to or devolved to local level for strengthening communities.

Policies: The strategy would benefit from a number of policy statements being integrated into it, such as a policy on asset transfer of underused public buildings to community management or ownership. It would also benefit from a clear statement of support for voluntary sector infrastructure organisations and the key CCB roles they carry out.

Action plan: An action plan section in the strategy would need a set of objectives and targets for the next three to five years and a proposed method of assessing progress and success. The action plan will need actions to ensure minority groups are not excluded from CCB activities. Finally, the strategy would benefit from a description of how different partner organisations will be involved.

Partners will have different parts to play in the implementation of such a strategy. Developing a strategy on stronger communities will need to involve the effective participation of the community and voluntary sectors, with their representatives being fully involved in its production. For public service managers, this involvement may mean a cultural shift to really listen to the voices from the grass roots and to be prepared to take on board different perspectives. A partnership overseeing such a strategic initiative will itself need to involve effective listening by all stakeholders, including by representatives of the community and voluntary sectors.

A strategic approach to CCB needs to consider the issues raised in Chapter 5 on *building equality*, since without a strong position on values, the strategy will not be fit for purpose. As mentioned above, the strategy can also highlight both the needs and strengths of *communities of interest*, and of *communities of place*, especially deprived areas and neighbourhoods. In other words, it is not a case of one at the cost of the other, but rather both types of communities being part of an effective strategy.

The discussion so far in this chapter on a strategic approach to strengthening communities has focused on CCB – community capacity building. This addresses the first three of the seven key features of the definition of strong communities: *active, participative and organised.* As described in Chapter 1, the scope of this book is mainly on these first three features. Addressing the other four key features would require a much broader strategy, covering, for example, issues such as community cohesion.

Box 6.2 Civil society strategy

In 2018, the government launched a new strategy called 'Civil Society Strategy: Building a Future that Works for Everyone'. The strategy aims to create places where local communities take more responsibility for where they live. As part of this, government aims to improve guidance to help communities take ownership of local assets. As well as enhancing existing opportunities, it includes the launch of a new 'Innovation in Democracy' programme that will pilot ways for people to take a more direct role in decisions that affect them. This could be through citizens' juries or participation in online polls. The strategy's focus is on charities and social enterprises, to encourage them to have a strong role in shaping policy. Regarding the public sector, the aim here is to encourage more 'collaborative commissioning', so that voluntary organisations are involved in a meaningful way in creating and delivering public services. It promotes an increase in 'social value commissioning' across all levels of government. The report states:

> 'The government recognises that all places are not all starting from the same point. The factors that distinguish communities from one another, such as levels of deprivation and segregation, will affect a community's ability to take greater control. The government will take steps to ensure that efforts to support communities described in this Strategy have the potential to benefit all communities, regardless of circumstance.'

> (HM Government, 2018, p. 3)

At the time of writing it is difficult to comment on the likely impact of the new strategy.

Organising agency capacity building

The focus so far has been on public sector organisations getting involved in activities and programmes to support community-based capacity building. However, public service providers also need to take on board the idea of building their own capacity to effectively engage with the community and voluntary sectors. The term *agency capacity building* is useful here to highlight that learning and development needs to happen equally in the public sector, not just in communities. Therefore, as well as looking outwards to support community groups and activities, public sector organisations also need to look inwards at their own staff abilities and organisational culture. The four headings explored in earlier chapters can also be applied to *agency capacity building* for public sector organisations. These four themes are now looked at from a different angle – rather than focused on support in the community, they are now used to explore areas of professional development and organisational change in public sector organisations.

Building people

Building people can involve public sector organisations looking at the professional development of their front-line staff and service managers so that they can more effectively engage with and support communities. *Building people* could also strengthen the roles of elected members to act as community leaders, as introduced in Chapter 2 and discussed further in Resource Three below.

Staff and managers involved in front-line services and area management will already be bringing a wide range of skills and abilities to contribute to strengthening communities. This valuable resource can be further developed through learning programmes, focusing, for example, on their:

➤ *Skills base* – developing skills in community engagement methods; the practice of community development; addressing barriers to participation.

➤ *Knowledge base* – such as knowledge of funding sources, how the council works, how community groups operate or what valuing diversity means.

➤ *Qualities* – such as a 'can-do' attitude or having a problem-solving approach.

➤ *Understanding* – of the voluntary and community sectors; diversity, inclusion and equal opportunities; community empowerment.

Box 6.3 Introducing VOiCE

A key resource for effective engagement is called VOiCE, which stands for Visioning Outcomes in Community Engagement. It has been developed by the Scottish Community Development Centre and supported by the Scottish Government to implement the National Standards for Community Engagement. VOiCE is planning and recording software that assists individuals, organisations and partnerships to design and deliver effective community engagement. The system will enable use of

▶

◄

a common approach for analysing, planning, monitoring, evaluating and recording community engagement. VOiCE will support users to reflect on what they are trying to achieve, develop plans that relate to their purpose, and monitor progress in implementing their plan. It also supports the evaluation of the process and outcomes and learning lessons for future activity.

Building organisations

Public service providers will also need to look at how they are organised and to consider changes that may strengthen their abilities to engage with and support communities. Many are already dedicated to effective interaction with communities through user panels, area committees and neighbourhood forums. This valuable resource of experience can be built on by *changing the organisational culture* so that it is more open to community engagement. This may mean, for example, accepting that valid consultation could require additional time for community representatives to give feedback to their networks for views on key decisions before they are taken. Equally important is the *changing of structures* – looking at how the public service organisation itself is structured, and whether this supports CCB and participation in decision-making. One way to organise this is through increased use of what are called *area-based arrangements*.

Public sector organisations have a number of choices in how they organise themselves to engage with and support communities. At neighbourhood, town or ward level, different structures for engagement can be established with differing types of outcomes. Local government is usually the setting for these types of arrangements, though much of the material now discussed will be relevant to other public service providers, such as social housing providers.

Area-based arrangements can be set up to cover a specific town, group of villages, neighbourhood, ward, number of wards or whole local authority area. They can be led by elected members, council officers, other public organisations or residents. They may involve public and voluntary sector services working together who also involve residents and community representatives. In some cases, area arrangements involve decision-making over local issues and devolved budgets.

Within these different possibilities, there are five different *types* of local arrangements, and some local arrangements can be seen as more empowering and involving than others. These five types can be summarised using the following short sentences:

➢ *Type One – 'We'll try to sort your problems out'.*

➢ *Type Two – 'We want to hear your views'.*

➤ *Type Three – 'We want to involve you in decisions'.*

➤ *Type Four – 'We want to work with you'.*

➤ *Type Five – 'We want to be part of your community activities'.*

More detailed information is given in Resource Four below. The five types are adapted from valuable research carried out by Richardson and Durose (2013). In addition, recent research indicates that a new model of neighbourhood management has emerged in response to the current economic climate. Instead of seeing area-based arrangements as being limited to deprived areas and special funding opportunities, there is evidence to show that it is becoming much more extensive in its geographical coverage and ambitious in the range of issues it addresses. This broader approach is called 'strategic locality working' and is being coordinated across multiple agencies. The research indicates strategic locality working is transforming services at the neighbourhood level (Houghton, 2018).

Building involvement

Many public service providers are already involving communities in a variety of ways and supporting increased influence on decisions that affect people's lives at local levels. This needs to be enhanced through more effective community engagement and decision-making *systems.* Often engagement methods are used by public bodies without careful consideration of aims. For public services, the Ladder of Participation is a useful framework to better understand and plan for effective community involvement in decision-making. The Ladder describes levels of community involvement and influence, presented as a range of opportunities or 'rungs'. Wilcox's research-based version has been widely used by the public sector and communities to understand relationships in community engagement. The Ladder of Participation is described further in Resource Five. An important resource is also the National Community Engagement Standards, developed in Scotland: www.scdc.org.uk/what/national-standards. Further guidelines on community empowerment and a useful set of principles to support interested public services in on www.audit-scotland.gov.uk

Building equality

Many public sector organisations are addressing equality issues in their policies and procedures and some have led the way in being innovative and forward thinking. Such constructive initiatives can be extended to inform how organisations engage with communities. For example, public sector organisations can set up specific forums for marginalised groups and appoint a lead 'champion', a senior manager who helps to ensure such issues are kept on the agenda. As discussed, as well as focusing on communities of place, CCB can also highlight the needs and strengths of communities of interest, especially those marginalised or excluded from mainstream service provision. Particular issues to consider include: Will reductions in budgets for CCB and neighbourhood management affect poorer areas and marginalised groups more than the mainstream? Can anti-discriminatory practices and policies developed within public sector organisations be applied to front-line services? Are men given greater opportunities than women to act as community representatives? Does the organisational culture of front-line service teams promote diversity and inclusion?

A coordinated approach

This chapter has focused on three key elements of strategic planning:

➢ Providing community capacity building support

➢ Developing a joint strategy on strengthening communities

➢ Organising agency capacity building.

In combination, these three headings provide a framework for public sector organisations to use in developing new procedures, structures and processes that support the strengthening of communities. Organisational change ideally needs to happen simultaneously at a number of levels, involving front-line workers, unit teams, departments and senior strategic bodies. Senior management needs to give the lead, based on a long-term, strategic approach. It may involve shifts in organisational culture so that public service providers are more open to working with different sectors and with community-led organisations.

These three different approaches to strengthening communities need to be coordinated between different stakeholders, rather than be a set of silo initiatives. Coordination needs to involve representatives from both voluntary and community sectors. For such partnership working to be effective, all partner organisations, especially public services, will need to develop a solid understanding of the processes of strengthening communities, maintaining information flows between members, and accessing any additional funding.

Practitioners have key roles to play in building and maintaining partnerships that support strengthening communities, for instance, discussing the value of a strategic approach with key stakeholders and political leaders. It may involve bringing together different partners and sectors to produce a joint strategy on strengthening communities. It can also mean ensuring community representatives have real opportunities to contribute to and influence decisions. Partnership working in the UK has a mixed history, where in many cases the community involvement has been limited to token representation, and has been diverted into the 'wrong game', that is, into participation in networks that are not the real centres of power and decision-making (Taylor, 2003).

Box 6.4 Barriers to community empowerment

A report published by Locality identified a range of barriers to community empowerment:

- *Top-down decision-making*: When communities cannot access the real centres of decision-making, local initiative and confidence can be frustrated.

- *Risk aversion and lack of trust*: Public sector leaders may be too cautious and consequently be less prepared to work with communities.

- *Narrow participation*: Engagement is dominated by the strongest voices.

- *Lack of control over funding and resources*: Systems and procedures make access to resources difficult for community groups.

- *Accountability deficit*: Engagement is limited to basic methods of voting and consultations.

- *Lack of access to data and information*: Participants wish to contribute to decision-making but cannot access the information needed.

(Adapted from Locality, 2017)

Some community groups, networks and representatives may not wish to participate in partnerships with much larger and more powerful organisations. They may fear that policies controlling resources will limit the scope for effective community influence (Taylor, 2003). Facing such barriers, some groups may not want to be part of a partnership approach but choose other methods of activity and engagement. Another concern is that community representatives sitting on partnership boards become drawn into the agenda and limitations of the partnership, rather than maintaining their community's priorities (Purdue et al., 2000).

For practitioners, there will be a number of challenges when working in a partnership context. They may be liaising with more senior people in organisations and themselves feel marginalised. They can be wrongly viewed as the voice of the community sector and end up doing only what they think needs doing, rather than reflecting the needs of communities (Twelvetrees, 2017). Managers in public sector organisations will also encounter a range of challenges, such as having to understand different operating styles between sectors. Officers may be reluctant to share their power and be unfamiliar with liaising with other agencies (Clark, 1999). Deadlines for consultation may need to be extended so that community representatives can report back to their own networks. Equally, more recent concerns are about the time and resources involved in maintaining partnerships and associated networks. However, overall, partnership working to develop stronger communities is essential and worth the investment of time and resources.

Summary

Chapter 6 has introduced some key material on building partnerships; it looked at:

> What is involved in partnership working for strengthening communities;

> How public services can support CCB programmes and activities;

> A range of key elements needed for an effective strategy on strengthening communities;

> The idea of area arrangements; and

> The Ladder of Participation as a useful framework for community involvement in decision-making.

Key points have been:

> The four key headings of *building organisations*, *building people*, *building involvement* and *building equality* can be used by public services in organising support for strengthening communities.

> A strategy on strengthening communities needs to be firmly based on the values of equal opportunities, diversity and inclusion.

> Choosing an appropriate type of area-based arrangement is central for strengthening communities at local level.

> Initiatives to support strengthening communities need coordination between partners.

The focus of this book has been on strengthening communities through working with and empowering the grass roots. This approach acknowledges that empowerment cannot be given but that practitioners can support and develop opportunities and situations where communities can discover, create and win their own empowerment. The emphasis has been on starting from strengths to build confidence and effective involvement. Underpinning all activities and policies must be a firm values base including supporting equal opportunities, valuing diversity and promoting inclusion. It is difficult work, and real changes are often not obvious. It's great that you are interested and have read this far! I hope this book has inspired you to work with communities to help to create a fairer world.

(Steve Skinner, 2019)

Resources

www.scdc.org.uk/what/national-standards/
www.salfordcvs.co.uk/little-hulton-big-local
www.voicescotland.org.uk/voice/
www.cles.org.uk/tag/the-preston-model
www.localneighbourhood.org/wp-content/uploads/2018/07/Doing-the-right-thing
www.audit-scotland.gov.uk

References: Chapter 6

Cahn, E. (2001) *No More Throw-away People: The Co-Production Imperative.* Washington, DC: Essential Books.

Chanan, G. (2002) *Measures of Community.* London: Community Development Foundation.

Chanan, G. and Fisher, B. (2017) *Commissioning Community Development for Health: A Concise Handbook.* London: Coalition for Collaborative Care and the Health Empowerment Leverage Project (HELP).

Clark, C. (1999) *Effective Partnerships for Managers and Board Members.* London: The Civic Trust.

HM Government. (2018) *Civil Society Strategy: Building a Future that Works for Everyone – Executive Summary.* London: HM Government.

Houghton, J. (2018) *Doing the Right Thing.* London: National Association for Neighbourhood Management.

Johnson, G., Scholes, K. and Whittington, R. (2008) *Fundamentals of Strategy.* Harlow: Prentice Hall.

NCVO. (2015) *UK Civic Society Almanac.* London: NCVO.

Parsfield, M., Morris, D., Bola, M., Knapp, M., Yoshioka, M. and Marcus, G. (2015) *Community Capital: The Value of Connected Communities.* London: Royal Society of Arts.

Purdue, D., Razzaque, K., Hambleton, R. and Stewart, M. (2000) *Community Leadership in Area Regeneration.* Bristol: Policy Press.

Richardson, E. and Durose, C. (2013) *Who is Accountable in Localism?*. Birmingham: University of Birmingham.

Skinner, S. (1997) *Building Community Strengths*. London: Community Development Foundation.

Skinner, S. (2006) *Strengthening Communities: A Guide to Capacity Building for Communities and the Public Sector*. London: Community Development Foundation.

Taylor, M. (2003) *Public Policy in the Community*. London: Red Globe Press.

Twelvetrees, A. (2017) *Community Development, Social Action and Social Planning*. London: Red Globe Press.

Resource One

Definitions

All the definitions given below were devised by the author and published in earlier works, unless indicated (Skinner, 1997 and 2006).

Capacity Building is a process of learning and change that increases the ability of individuals and organisations to contribute to the development of communities.

However, it is useful to identify two different versions within this general definition:

> *Community capacity building* means activities, resources and support that strengthen the skills, abilities and confidence of people and groups to take effective action and leading roles in the development of communities.

> *Agency capacity building* is learning, resources and organisational change that increases the ability of public sector organisations to engage with communities effectively.

The Community Sector is the whole range of autonomous collective and group activity, directly undertaken by individuals within their neighbourhood or community of interest to improve the quality of life.

(Chanan et al., 1999)

The Voluntary Sector is made up of organisations whose activities are carried out other than for profit, but which are not public or local authorities. The organisations are usually formally constituted and may employ professional and administrative staff. They may or may not use volunteer help (Home Office, 2004).

There are two features that help to distinguish between voluntary sector and community sector organisations:

> *Size* – Generally the community sector is made up of a large number of small-scale organisations and groups, who often do not have paid staff. One definition, for example, suggested any group with less than two staff or equivalent is a part of the community sector (Chanan, 2002).

> *Control* – Community sector groups and organisations are usually run mainly by their individual members, users or local residents. In contrast, many larger voluntary organisations have management committees or boards made up predominantly of professionals from public services, other voluntary organisations, local businesses or the council.

These features vary and are based on generalisations. There are also exceptions, for example, where resident-led organisations have obtained funding to employ a team of staff, as has happened in some Big Local Partnerships.

References: Resource One

Chanan, G. (2002) *Measures of Community.* London: Community Development Foundation.

Chanan, G., West, A., Garrett, C. and Humm, J. (1999) *Regeneration and Sustainable Communities.* London: Community Development Foundation.

Skinner, S. (1997) *Building Community Strengths.* London: Community Development Foundation.

Skinner, S. (2006) *Strengthening Communities: A Guide to Capacity Building for Communities and the Public Sector.* London: Community Development Foundation.

Resource Two

Skills for community representatives

Research carried out for the National Association for Voluntary and Community Action (NAVCA) identified three main sets of skills being used by community representatives. The research focused on representatives' involvement in district-wide, strategic partnerships. These notes draw on the research findings.

People skills

Acting assertively

- Give your own views confidently and directly in ways that maintain effective relationships.
- Display calmness, courage and persistence in standing up for third sector interests.
- Propose and challenge in ways that persuades and inspires others.
- Say no to unreasonable requests.
- Encourage assertiveness in others in the partnership.
- Display belief in own role and contributions.

Being self-aware

- Understand the impact of personal communication style on others.
- Review your own practice.
- Seek opportunities for personal and professional development.
- Maintain openness and ability to change.
- Know when you're out of depth on issues.
- Be honest.

Problem-solving

➢ Identify and work around blocks to achieve progress.

➢ Learn quickly in new situations.

➢ Use creative approaches to generate new ideas and solutions.

➢ Adopt a positive attitude to change.

➢ Translate theory into practice.

Using political skills

➢ Anticipate the impact of your own views and actions on others.

➢ Employ tact and diplomacy while maintaining integrity and honesty.

➢ Maintain balance between challenging and cooperating to achieve goals.

➢ Choose the right approach for the right moment.

➢ Work with the power bases within the partnership.

➢ Display awareness of political structures and personal agendas.

Enabling others

➢ Build understanding in groups and networks of the roles of representatives.

➢ Encourage others to become representatives as appropriate.

➢ Seek to reduce barriers to participation.

➢ Help to develop other people's confidence and skills in representation.

➢ Seek to understand other people's needs and motivations.

Practical skills

Being organised

➢ Manage your own time as a resource.

➢ Plan ahead for key meetings and deadlines.

➢ Use IT to support your work.

➢ Display reliability and consistency in keeping to practical arrangements.

Communicating

- ➤ Present information clearly, concisely, accurately and in ways that promote understanding.
- ➤ Ensure your own advice and views are supported by reasoned argument and appropriate evidence.
- ➤ Ensure formal and informal presentations are informed and creative.
- ➤ Relate positively to people from diverse backgrounds and sectors.
- ➤ Use listening skills to develop effective relationships.

Accessing and using knowledge

- ➤ Manage and use different forms of information and data.
- ➤ Scan and select from large amounts of information.
- ➤ Analyse information to identify useful points and key findings.
- ➤ Apply specialist subject knowledge to different situations and contexts.
- ➤ Use opportunities appropriately to share your own knowledge with others.

Negotiating

- ➤ Develop productive working relationships with partners.
- ➤ Identify desired outcomes in negotiating processes.
- ➤ Use planning and tactics effectively.
- ➤ Achieve objectives and desired outcomes.

Mediating

- ➤ Seek understanding of opposing positions.
- ➤ Reduce tensions between parties.
- ➤ Facilitate fairly between people with conflicting needs.
- ➤ Encourage win-win solutions.

Partnership skills

Representing

➤ Keep up to date with local issues, drawing information and resources from a range of national and local sources.

➤ Build understanding of what community representatives do.

➤ Act in an accountable way as representative.

➤ Promote the interests of the whole third sector when appropriate.

Feeding back

➤ Ensure systematic feedback to community networks and groups.

➤ Maintain close contact and links with local groups and networks.

➤ Consult with groups and networks on key issues and decisions.

➤ Ensure minorities are part of the feedback communication networks.

Joint working

➤ Seek to understand partner organisations' needs, resources and motivations.

➤ Develop an overview across sectors to achieve common goals.

➤ Constructively challenge proposals when needed, and seek better alternatives.

➤ Build trust and credibility in relationships with partners and the third sector.

Being strategic

➤ Develop understanding of the partnership's aims and resources.

➤ Apply understanding of community issues.

➤ Balance long-term goals with short-term activities to achieve aims.

➤ Promote use of resources to achieve long-term objectives.

➤ Display understanding of the big picture and the long term.

Using values

➤ Ensure diversity and equality of opportunity are addressed in policies and programmes.

➤ Ensure social inclusion in the development of the partnership.

➤ Model behaviour that shows respect, assertiveness and openness.

➤ Promote inclusive and empowering ways of working within communities.

(Adapted from Skinner and Mitchell, 2008)

References: Resource Two

Skinner, S. and Mitchell, L. (2008) *Skilling Up for Stronger Voices*. Sheffield: NAVCA.

Resource Three

Elected members as community leaders

The current economic climate throws up many challenges for front-line ward members, requiring relationships with communities that may be different from the more traditional ones. One way of describing this is seeing the ward member as a 'community leader', where leadership can be described as a set of six roles. The six roles, initially introduced in Chapter 2 and now expanded on below, were devised by the author through discussion over several years with a wide range of councillors and officers as part of the Local Government Information Unit's seminar series on community engagement. The six roles also draw on a useful framework of political skills developed by the Local Government Association (Silvester, 2013).

The six roles are:

➢ enabling decision-making

➢ enabling action

➢ building bridges

➢ managing local resources

➢ joint working

➢ enhancing community capacity.

The six roles can be treated as a 'menu' to be drawn from and are additional to, rather than in any way replacing, the more traditional political roles of the front-line ward member. The focus here is on community leadership at local level, rather than at corporate level. The six roles are now explored.

Role One: Enabling decision-making

Central to effective community engagement is the process of local people getting involved in decision-making on issues that affect them. The types of decisions at local level may be about:

➢ a local service, such as the council's waste collection

➤ a local issue or problem, such as isolation amongst older people

➤ a local resource, such as the use of an empty public building.

Necessary decisions may also be:

➤ short term, such as concerning the use of a library building that is having to close soon, or

➤ longer term, such as priorities for a Neighbourhood Plan.

For many elected members, *enabling decision-making* is a challenging role, very different from the more traditional approach of acting as a political representative who speaks for and decides as a council member on behalf of others. However, enabling community involvement in decision-making can help to increase ownership by residents of local initiatives. If done well, it can raise levels of satisfaction about local services.

For this involvement to be meaningful, it is important for councillors to explain to members of communities in what ways they can or cannot influence a decision. This role will involve letting people know the extent of influence they can have, for example, whether it is a joint decision they can make with councillors or a consultation about a decision that ward councillors, or the council executive committee or 'cabinet' will make themselves at a later point. Either way, in order for local people to effectively participate in decision-making, they will need an appropriate level of information given to them, made available in an accessible and timely manner.

Role Two: Enabling action

Many elected members are involved in regular casework, where individual residents notify them about issues of concern about local services or the area. Usually with such casework, the elected member then takes action to address the issue, for example, by contacting the relevant council service manager. In addition to casework, the councillor can sometimes act as an enabler to support groups and residents to take action themselves to solve local problems.

Such *enabling action* can take a number of different forms, including:

➤ helping groups translate good ideas into action

➤ putting community groups in touch with officers

➤ providing information, for example on funding sources

➤ clarifying tasks that need to be carried out

➤ sharing tasks with people, rather than doing it all yourself

➤ providing practical support to people with less confidence

➤ in some cases, taking initiatives to show what can be done

➤ asking challenging questions to push things along

➤ chasing up on agreed actions to ensure they are happening.

In practice, it will often be a combination of members doing things them-selves and enabling others to do things.

Role Three: Building bridges

This role is about helping stronger relationships to form between groups and organisations at area level. Such links can increase understanding of differ-ences and help communities to get on better.
    This role could include:

➤ encouraging contact and shared activities between community groups, especially where groups may have different faiths or identities, for example a Hindu community group based in a mainly white neighbourhood

➤ supporting informal networks of community groups and joint working between groups

➤ involving parish, town and community councils, local businesses and vol-untary organisations in local initiatives

➤ making contacts with groups of people who may often be left out and marginalised, for example due to low levels of mobility

➤ acting as a mediator to build better relationships between different groups

➤ ensuring that contact information on groups in the area, with their approval, is made available through newsletters, directories and websites.

Building bridges is about building links to achieve better understanding and increased community cohesion.

Role Four: Managing local resources

Councillors can get involved in *managing local resources* in various ways such as:

➤ sitting on management committees of community centres or locally based voluntary organisations

➤ becoming a school governor

➢ deciding with colleagues on the use of a small grants budget to fund community activities

➢ encouraging the use of under-used 'assets', such as buildings and land that could be used for community benefit

➢ contributing to decisions on the use of funding, such as the Community Infrastructure Levy.

In practice, *managing local resources* will require a balancing act by councillors as they will need to consider a variety of needs in the area, combined with considerations of the authority's wider policies and aims.

Role Five: Joint working

This role involves bringing together people from community groups, public services, voluntary organisations and businesses to improve the quality of services in the area. Such initiatives may take the form of a partnership with a forward plan, or it may act more informally as a network.

Joint working is about the better coordination of local services to ensure value for money, and the emphasis should always be about people and organisations coming together to get things done. Many public and voluntary sector organisations will be committed to community engagement and can be valuable partners, appreciating the opportunity to work jointly with the local authority.

The councillor's role in *joint working* might involve chairing or facilitating meetings and ensuring agreed actions are carried out. In many cases, working jointly can have substantial impact merely by strengthening the levels of coordination between a range of service providers, even in times of reducing budgets.

Joint working focuses on local services, whereas *enabling action* is more about supporting community-led initiatives and action.

Role Six: Enhancing community capacity

Achieving real change in an area will need to involve many people, groups and organisations in new challenges, projects and initiatives. Many active residents, volunteers, community leaders and community groups are themselves aware that in order to do this it will often require building on their existing skills and abilities. Examples of the types of skills needed in community action, enterprise and self-help are:

➢ the management of money, assets and resources

➢ planning new projects

➢ fundraising and accessing resources

➢ teamwork and committee skills

➢ entrepreneurial behaviours, risk taking and problem-solving

➢ presentation skills

➢ being accountable to the community

➢ knowledge of how local authorities work

➢ evaluation skills.

Often such skills already exist in communities and groups to some degree, but they are under-used; *enhancing community capacity* can be partly about helping people to value and use their existing skills and knowledge.

Enhancing community capacity is about supporting and strengthening local leadership and groups so that communities are well-organised and take responsibility, and so that their available talents and skills can be put to good use. For example, by participating in a training programme, a residents' association may then be in a position to manage their own community centre more effectively, thus keeping a local service going.

Enhancing community capacity can also involve:

➢ helping active citizens and groups to participate in learning activities, such as training courses

➢ sharing information, skills and experience

➢ encouraging community enterprise and self-help

➢ helping to build local organisations, charities and trusts that can act as catalysts for long-term change

➢ ensuring training and learning opportunities for local groups are open to all groups, not just those already well established.

Using the six roles

This set of roles can help elected members to build stronger communities in their areas. It is not proposed that any one member needs to carry out all of these six roles; the set of six roles is presented as a menu to choose from, depending on abilities, preferences and local needs.

However, as a framework, the six roles can be used by elected members, with support from officers, to look at how to plan their work over the coming year. Some further points to consider are:

➢ Some areas may lack opportunities for people to have a say about local decisions and need support around *enabling decision-making*.

> Some areas may already have effective coordination between services, so need less support in *joint working*.

> Others may have a lack of links between different community groups and need help with *building bridges*.

Each area will have a different combination of needs, and elected members will rightly have their own styles and priorities.

So, the six roles can be used to:

> help councillors plan their priorities for the coming year

> support officers to understand more fully what their councillors are doing in the community

> develop a policy on member development and involvement

> help councillors and officers make choices about the community engagement methods they use.

In focusing their activities more as community leaders, some members may fear it will increase their workload. However, as described, *enabling action* will often involve sharing tasks, rather than an elected member always directly doing things themselves. Thus, *enhancing community capacity* should, in the longer term, increase the level of leadership and resources in an area, as new people come forward to get involved, and as under-used skills and energies are made use of.

The six roles are a resource to draw on and to be used in a flexible way. They are not in any way intended as a substitute for the existing roles that members have as political representatives of their wards, involving core political skills. The Local Government Association's useful toolkit on the Political Skills Framework describes these (Silvester, 2013).

Used creatively, the six roles can support councillors in their relationships with their communities. They reflect a growing consensus about local democracy and the valuable part elected members have to play as local leaders in engaging with communities.

The 21st Century Councillor

The 21st Century Councillor, published by the University of Birmingham (Mangan et al., 2016), describes how councillor roles are adapting to contextual challenges. Based on their research, key roles for the future include:

> Steward of place – working across the locality in partnership with others

> Advocate – acting to represent the interests of all citizens

➢ Buffer – seeking to mitigate the impact of austerity on citizens

➢ Sense-maker – translating a shift in the role of public services and the relationship between institutions and citizens

➢ Catalyst – enabling citizens to do things for themselves, and having new conversations about what is now possible

➢ Entrepreneur – working with citizens and partners to encourage local vitality and develop new solutions

➢ Orchestrator – helping broker relationships, work with partners and develop new connections.

This research-based publication provides very useful insights into the roles of councillors. Some of them overlap with those in the set of six community leadership roles described above, such as catalyst and orchestrator; others add additional and valuable perspectives on the range of roles being carried out.

References: Resource Three

Mangan, C., Needham, C., Bottom, K. and Parker, S. (2016) *The 21st Century Councillor*. Birmingham: University of Birmingham.
Silvester, J. (2013) *The Political Skills Framework: A Councillor's Toolkit*. London: LGA.

Resource Four

Establishing area-based arrangements

This section describes five types of area arrangement for public services, focusing mainly on local authorities. Some local authorities have adopted area-based arrangements spread across the whole city or district, while others have used such arrangements only in targeted areas of deprivation. For local authorities, the benefits and outcomes for each type of arrangement will vary, as discussed below. A key question is which arrangement will contribute in that particular setting more effectively to strengthen local communities.

Different types of area arrangements

Type One – regular public meetings are held across the area, chaired by councillors or service managers, where residents can raise concerns about local services and issues. Some local authorities call these *'neighbourhood forums'*. The concerns raised by the public are normally recorded and, where appropriate, actions then are taken by the council to address them, with a report back on progress at the next meeting. The meetings may also be attended by managers from other public services. Type One arrangements are essentially a mechanism for public service providers to receive and act on complaints and comments on its services. Type One is a fairly common arrangement for local authorities and a useful way to address local concerns. People participate by individually raising their concerns and commenting on local services from their perspective. Type One arrangements tend to maintain an expectation by residents that the council will do things for the community, rather than encouraging a joint approach to problem-solving. The overall relationship with the community, reflected in Type One, can be summed up as:

'We'll try to sort your problems out'.

➤ *Type Two* – an area-based committee made up of ward councillors that has delegated powers from the council executive to make decisions on a specific range of local services, such as the management of parks. It consults the local community and service providers on its decisions. The consultations may be organised through regularly held public meetings or be based on other methods, such as a local survey or by using social media. Rather than just receiving complaints and concerns as in Type One, Type Two arrangements involve consultation with the local community in a more systematic way and can use delegated powers to make a certain range of decisions locally. These powers are often related to 'visible' services, such as the parks and the environment. In Type Two, the councillors essentially make their own decisions about local issues but consult on residents' views beforehand.

'We want to hear your views'.

➤ *Type Three* – an area-based committee made up of ward councillors that has delegated decision-making powers from the council executive and also involves a number of representatives from the community and voluntary sectors in jointly making certain local decisions. The focus is on involving a defined number of people as community representatives in decision-making on local issues. As in Type Two, Type Three requires approval from the Council Executive for a certain level of decision-making power for Council members to use at local level. As well as involving community representatives, such a body may also consult more widely on local issues. This arrangement can also involve managers from a range of public services.

'We want to involve you in decisions'.

➤ *Type Four* – a locally based partnership, network or open forum of service providers, community group representatives and active residents that is *facilitated* by councillors or council officers to coordinate local projects and support community activities. Participation is not limited to a specified number of identified community representatives but to anyone who attends the meetings. Type Four could take the form of a local partnership or network of groups and public services and be much less formal in how it is organised compared to Types One, Two and Three. A key feature is that membership from the local community is completely open to whoever is interested, as opposed, for example, to Type Three, where it is limited to selected or elected community representatives. The emphasis in Type Four is on community action and communities tackling problems themselves, rather than the focus being mostly about improved services. In Type Four, elected members may have fewer active roles, though still have a key contribution to make as facilitators.

'We want to work with you'.

➤ *Type Five* – a locally based partnership, network or open forum, made up of and often led by community groups, community leaders and active residents. Councillors and council officers *participate* on an equal basis to join existing activities and jointly decide on local priorities. Type Five will be more community led and usually take the form of a network or partnership and can also involve coordination of local projects and support for community activities. Type Five could be either established by a local authority or initiated by the local community. It may well start as a network focusing on a single issue, but over time may expand to include a wider range of interests. Elected members and council officers, whilst giving practical support, will have no particular or special role to play as facilitators or chairs. They may provide advice, contacts and information but essentially participate as equal members of the network or partnership.

'We want to be part of your community activities'.

These different types of local arrangements draw on a similar set devised by Richardson and Durose (2018), based on their valuable research. They were adapted and developed by the author over several years through consultation with officers and councillors participating in community engagement training sessions.

Area arrangements and building stronger communities

In order to work towards creating stronger communities, some types of local arrangements, such as Types Three, Four and Five, are likely to have greater impact and help to generate community activity, enterprise and self-help than others. With Types Three, Four and Five, councillors and officers need to behave with more flexibility and less formal processes. In this context, their role may be more one of facilitation rather than of taking control. Some local authorities are interested in Type Five arrangements, which have strong features of collective decision-making and joint action to achieve agreed goals. Here responsibility may be more shared, with local community action initiatives and projects being seen as contributing to joint efforts to improve the area. This approach is not necessarily so much about reducing resource use but about enabling better use of local budgets, officer time, skills and assets, in combination with the council's other service provision, in order to have greater impact on community life.

In making choices about area arrangements, communities, councils and public service providers will need to balance the desired outcomes with the level of resources needed. Whatever the structure chosen in establishing an area-based system, the public service providers will need to adopt a policy that clearly describes the function and decision-making powers of the local arrangements.

Ideally the choice of the type of arrangement set up in an area will itself involve the community; practitioners can have key roles to play in facilitating discussion across sectors and with different stakeholders. The range of types of local arrangements described above are useful for helping to clarify the intended outcomes. These are not the only five possibilities available; in practice, they may not be very distinct and there may often be a mixture of different options. Ideally, they need to be established in the context of a longer-term strategy for strengthening communities.

Questions for local authorities and communities to consider at an early stage are:

➢ What are our aims?

➢ Who defines the area?

➢ Who will be involved – anyone living in the area, or community represent-atives elected by local networks and groups?

➢ How large is the area to be covered by the local arrangement?

➢ What role would residents play in making decisions about local services and priorities?

➢ Could residents and community groups be supported to take more initia-tives and actions?

➢ How are parish councils, town or community councils involved?

➢ What resources will be available to resource any actions arising from issues dealt with and decisions made?

➢ How much council officer time is available to provide support?

➢ Is there a budget to pay for meetings and local events?

➢ How can we avoid too much officer time being used in a multitude of local initiatives?

➢ What arrangements will increase local initiatives and enhance community empowerment?

➢ How will local arrangements relate to the council's wider decision-making procedures?

➢ How can we ensure the focus is on action, not just talking?

➢ How will we measure our success?

In setting up local arrangements, these questions can be discussed with inter-ested stakeholders, such as residents' groups, other public services and volun-tary organisations based in the area.

Comparing the five types

The table gives some idea of the issues that may be associated with each of the five different types of local arrangements.

Type	Stance	Features	Issues
One	'We'll try to sort your problems out'.	Keeps accountability clear. Gives elected members a local presence.	Maintains the more traditional relationships of the council as the main provider of services. May not enhance community initiatives.
Two	'We want to hear your views'.	Useful as a way to enhance coordination between local services, making the best of what resources are available.	Communities are consulted but further involvement is not necessarily encouraged.
Three	'We want to involve you in decisions'.	Community representatives are involved in local decisions in a structured way.	As the community representatives are chosen by elected members, they may not be seen as accountable to the local community.
Four	'We want to work with you'.	Shifts relationships to where elected members act more as facilitators. May involve a wider range of people from the area.	Some elected members may find this a challenging environment.
Five	'We want to be part of your community activities'.	Shifts relationships to where elected members act more as participants. The main driver is the community, not the local authority. May involve a wider range of people from the area.	Can be too open-ended for effective coordination.

A key feature is that the level of influence and control held by public services and councillors generally declines from Type One to Type Five, whereas the level of influence held by some local people increases. Type One is essentially a method to trigger council-based action, and Type Two is primarily a mechanism for consultation, rather than joint decision-making or joint action. In contrast, in Type Five, councillors are involved as members or participants in a network, with no special status or role. The Good Lives Leeds scheme, in Leeds, West Yorkshire, is an interesting example of this.

Types One, Two and Three may also include the commissioning of some locally based services, using a delegated budget. This can have much appeal, though it may itself increase costs due to the level of officer support needed, therefore creating challenging demands during times of reduced budgets. Despite this, some authorities, such as Barnsley Council, have gone ahead with such arrangements, due to the perceived longer-term advantages.

The key feature of Type Three is that the ward or area committee involves representatives from the community, not just in a process of consultation on their views but directly in the decision-making process. It shows a shift in relationships, where councillors include community groups or local leaders as equal partners. As discussed in Chapter 3, community representatives can be seen as people who in some way have a 'voice' from the community or 'reflect' the area. This could be because they:

➤ live there and know it well

➤ are typical of the membership of some groups in the area

➤ can gather information on local views

➤ have been elected or selected by local community groups.

In participating in arrangements for Type Three, some elected members may feel resistant to sharing decision-making powers with 'community representatives'. After all: *'Was not I elected to represent the area?'* Others welcome working with community reps, seeing the local leadership they provide as a valuable resource that can contribute to problem-solving and joint working. Types Four and Five move further away from a 'them and us' style of decision-making to a more collective system. They are usually less formal in style and may attract residents not interested in the other types of arrangement.

In practice, different arrangements can be combined. As shown in the example, as well as establishing Ward Alliances, Barnsley Council is also involved in 'neighbourhood networks'. Another variation is that some authorities have adopted a locally based arrangement specific to one ward or area in order to tackle particular problems and needs, rather than have a council-wide system. The following examples describe three of the five types in action. Overall, the framework of five different types of area arrangements creates ways of thinking about strengthening communities at local level.

Ward Alliances in Barnsley

An example of Type Three

In 2013 and 2014, Barnsley Metropolitan Borough Council set up a new structure of area-based working with the purpose of helping to achieve the

Council's strategic priority of building 'strong and resilient communities'. This led to the creation of six Area Councils covering the borough, each holding six meetings per year. These are formal meetings comprised of the Elected Members for the area. They are held in public with no direct public partici- pation, and the minutes are reported to Full Council. The Area Councils set priorities for their own areas and are involved in local performance manage- ment and influencing Borough-wide service planning. Since 2015, the Area Councils have been commissioning local services to address area priorities and holding them to account. The Area Council Commissioning Budget for the Borough is currently £2.1 million per year, allocated equally by the number of wards in each area. The aim is to meet the strategic needs of the area, make use of Barnsley-based organisations, encouraging volunteering and build community capacity by commissioning local services.

Barnsley Council has also established 19 Ward Alliances which comprise the Ward Members plus a minimum of six community representatives, chosen by the Ward Members. The community representatives have an equal say on deci- sions reached by the Alliance. These are drawn from individuals living or work- ing in the Ward and those with an interest in the effectiveness of the Ward. The meetings are not public or formal meetings of the council, and the minutes are not reported to council but to the relevant Area Council for information.

At time of writing, the Ward Alliances have a budget of £210,000 per year, split equally between the wards. This funding is used to 'seed fund' commu- nity groups and to encourage locally based social action and volunteering. As the next phase of development, both Area Councils and Ward Alliances are using these funds as match funding to pull in external grants.A governance framework provides a combination of the set, non-negotiable elements of the Ward Alliance arrangements, as well as recommended best practice. Ward Alliances can determine for themselves how they are adopted.

The purpose of the Ward Alliances is also to:

➤ Develop a ward plan to meet the vision and priorities and take collective ownership to deliver this plan, recognising and utilising all the assets avail- able in the Ward.

➤ Make arrangements to engage and consult the wider community in set- ting the Ward priorities and helping to deliver the ward plan.

➤ Ensure that the strengths, skills and assets of the Ward are developed to contribute to its sustainability.

➤ Use the ward plan and its priorities to inform the commissioning decisions made by the Area Council under which they sit.

To complement these area arrangements and harness the wealth of existing community assets, the authority is also helping to set up 'Neighbourhood

Networks' in each ward. These are 'virtual' networks hosted by a local community group, created by improving the communication and connectivity between local businesses, community groups, parish councils, school governors, youth groups, and so on in order to further support the community in providing activities and tackling local problems. This ensures that the best use is being made of available community assets and that groups are aware of and can support the ward priorities if they wish. Networks are also used to promote the work of local groups and to offer a consultation mechanism to enable statutory and voluntary and community sector organisations to reach a wider audience within a locality.

The London Borough of Hackney

An example of Type Four

Hackney Council has set up Ward Forums across the borough to involve local communities in joint action and to support self-help and community action. Their policy on area arrangements states the main aim of the new Ward Forums is for councillors and residents to collaborate on identifying issues of local interest together, considering ways of addressing them, then working locally to find solutions. The focus is on developing and delivering projects and activities, not on meetings. The Ward Forums are held two or three times per year in each ward and in a variety of different locations, rather than just in council-owned buildings. Through the forums, members and officers are involved in facilitation to:

➢ help communities to identify local priorities

➢ enable active citizens to work with their local community to help find solutions to local issues.

Hackney Council has been active in training both officers and elected members in engagement methods, building on their substantial local experience.

The Big Local Partnership, Little Hulton, Salford

An example of Type Five

Little Hulton is an area north of the city of Salford, consisting of five estates with a combined population of just over 17,000. A few years ago, the area had a reputation for crime, drug use, unemployment and health problems but also had many local groups and projects helping to improve things.

The Big Local Partnership covers the whole area; their vision is to unite Little Hulton as a community and to enhance the well-being of local people. The board is the key decision-making body of the partnership, which is made up of 14 local residents with a broad spread of backgrounds and ages. It receives support from Salford Community and Voluntary Services as a 'Local Trusted Organisation', who employ two members of staff to work for the partnership. Particular achievements so far have been developing a community hub located between the five estates, running a successful small grants process which supports both local community groups and business start-ups, and working with partners to develop a youth hub at Little Hulton Library.

The Big Local Board in Little Hulton is now looking ahead to creating a legacy project which would continue beyond the 10-year Big Local funding period. They are exploring investment in a local park and pavilion. As part of this exploration, a number of residents were employed on a community research project in order to identify local needs and inform the development of the park. The partnership also has a number of task groups that involve residents, local projects and public service providers. The Council's neighbourhood office has been actively supportive of the partnership from the early days and the local authority is a valuable member of the partnership, with a ward councillor being active on the board.

References: Resource Four

Richardson, E. and Durose, C. (2013) *Who is Accountable in Localism?*. Birmingham: University of Birmingham.

Resource Five

The Ladder of Participation

Originally, the Ladder of Participation was created by Arnstein (1969). However, Wilcox (1994) devised a different version which is now more widely used by the public sector and communities to understand relationships in community engagement. Wilcox's ladder was the basis for a 'Guide to Effective Participation', which was commissioned by the Joseph Rowntree Foundation, and intended for those managing participation processes, rather than for grass roots activists. This guide suggested that rather than seeing some levels, called 'stances', as better than others, it is a matter of 'horses for courses'. The issue is what degree of control the power holder – who is managing the participation process – wishes to offer to other stakeholders.

The stances in the Ladder of Participation are:

➤ *Information* – The least public service providers can do is tell people what is planned.

➤ *Consultation* – Public service providers offer a number of options and listen to the feedback they get.

➤ *Deciding together* – Public service providers encourage others to provide some additional ideas and options and join in deciding the best way forward.

➤ *Acting together* – Not only do different stakeholders decide together what is best, but they form a partnership to carry it out.

➤ *Supporting independent community initiatives* – Public service providers help others do what they want, perhaps within a framework of grants, advice and support provided by the resource holder.

The Guide to Effective Participation provided further explanation of when and where a stance might be appropriate, and what methods might be used, including how to support community initiatives. The ladder is mainly designed to inform power holders, rather than provide detailed guidance to people who are organising at community level. Although the 'stances' are not presented as a hierarchy, the metaphor of the ladder brings that to mind. The idea of a 'spectrum' of participation, developed by the International Association of Public Participation, aims to avoid this. See Resources below. The Ladder of Participation is an excellent tool to use with groups to help them explore the level of influence they can have at different rungs.   It can be used in combination with the Wheel of Participation because each framework has different uses.

References for Resource Five

Arnstein, S.R. (1969) *A Ladder of Citizen Participation.* Journal of the American Planning Association, 35 (4).
Wilcox, D. (1994) *The Guide to Effective Participation* and further materials on the Ladder of Participation is available on:
www.partnerships.org.uk/guide/index.htm
www.partnerships.org.uk/guide/frame.htm
www.partnerships.org.uk/guide/stance.htm

The Ladder as a spectrum:

www.sustainingcommunity.wordpress.com/2017/02/14/spectrum-of-public-participation/
www.medium.com/@RedheadSteph/re-imagining-the-iap2-spectrum-9d24afdc1b2e
www.socialpinpoint.com/blog/iap2-public-participation-spectrum-reflections/

Index

www.ingramcontent.com/pod-product-compliance
Lightning Source LLC
Chambersburg PA
CBHW080422270326
41929CB00018B/3119